Teach® Yourself

THE FINANCE COACH

Lindsey Byrne

First published in Great Britain in 2015 by Hodder and Stoughton.
An Hachette UK company.

Copyright © Lindsey Byrne 2015

The right of Lindsey Byrne to be identified as the Author of the Work has been asserted by her in accordance with the Copyright, Designs and Patents Act 1988.

Database right Hodder & Stoughton (makers)

The *Teach Yourself* name is a registered trademark of Hachette UK.

British Library Cataloguing in Publication Data: a catalogue record for this title is available from the British Library.

9781473611016

1

The publisher has used its best endeavours to ensure that any website addresses referred to in this book are correct and active at the time of going to press. However, the publisher and the author have no responsibility for the websites and can make no guarantee that a site will remain live or that the content will remain relevant, decent or appropriate.

The publisher has made every effort to mark as such all words which it believes to be trademarks. The publisher should also like to make it clear that the presence of a word in the book, whether marked or unmarked, in no way affects its legal status as a trademark.

Every reasonable effort has been made by the publisher to trace the copyright holders of material in this book. Any errors or omissions should be notified in writing to the publisher, who will endeavour to rectify the situation for any reprints and future editions.

Typeset by Cenveo® Publisher Services.

Printed and bound in Great Britain by CPI Group (UK) Ltd, Croydon, CR0 4YY.

John Murray Learning policy is to use papers that are natural, renewable and recyclable products and made from wood grown in sustainable forests. The logging and manufacturing processes are expected to conform to the environmental regulations of the country of origin.

Hodder & Stoughton Ltd
Carmelite House
50 Victoria Embankment
London EC4Y 0DZ
www.hodder.co.uk

CONTENTS

Part 3: Functional specifics

MEET THE COACH

Lindsey Byrne is the director of a training and consultancy business started in 2003. Over the years she has worked with clients ranging from small businesses to global plcs on analysis of financial statements, strategic planning, financial evaluation of business plans and investment appraisal.

Lindsey is a CIMA qualified accountant (ACMA) with an MBA from Warwick University. She has worked for a range of blue chip companies in financial roles including GEC plc/Marconi plc, EMI Records and Britvic Soft Drinks.

Working as a consultant and trainer, she has assisted many companies with business and financial planning, and with the evaluation of accounts and business plans of other companies (potential customers, suppliers and agents).

DISCLAIMER

This book should not be used as a substitute for obtaining professional advice and input when compiling your financial statements or when evaluating the business results of your company or others. The content of this book is generic and, whilst suggestions are made on financial matters, readers are encouraged to contact professionally qualified accounting, tax and legal specialists to obtain advice specific to their circumstances.

This book should also be treated as an outline for information only in relation to accounting. For detailed information readers should refer to the relevant accounting standards published by the UK FRC, the IASB or the US FASB. This book does not contain advice on accounting treatments and does not consider the particular legal or other regulatory requirements of specific countries or jurisdictions.

ACKNOWLEDGEMENTS

Any book on this subject will be the product of the author's exposure to and learning from many business experiences, business managers and finance experts.

Particular thanks must go to:

- Lisa Weaver; audit expert, author of *Managing the Transition to IFRS-Based Financial Reporting* and Aston University Teaching Fellow, for her chapter 'I've got an Audit Coming Up' (chapter 7),

- Robert Hope; Investor Relations Manager at Sky for his insights into the broadcast media industry,

- The BBC, ITV and Sky for their permissions to use their accounts as examples in this text,

- JSB Group Ltd and Hemsley Fraser Group Ltd for their contributions to content,

- Nick Byrne, my husband, for his moral support, proofreading, common-sense checking, good ideas and examples,

- And of course, Iain Campbell, my publisher, for all his support and Claire Handy, my editor, for her guidance and help.

HOW TO USE THIS BOOK

This book is intended as a practical, no no-nonsense guide to financial matters using plain English and structured around the specific financial questions that managers, business owners and individuals have in relation to their roles.

No matter what your function in business, you will have an impact on the financial results of your company; therefore, is important to understand the objectives of the company, the financial impact of your decisions and actions, and have some tools to plan and evaluate your future actions.

A greater financial understanding will allow you to communicate with:

- Your team: helping you to set meaningful targets that ensure everyone is pulling in the same direction.

- Your manager and/or finance colleagues: ensuring you negotiate an attainable budget that allows you to achieve your objectives or gain approval and funding for investments.

- Customers, potential customers and suppliers: giving them confidence in the financial stability of your business and your stewardship.

- Outside investors: to give them confidence in your planning and control of the business.

In this book we will answer a number of financial questions you may have: each chapter answers a specific question and can be read as a stand-alone chapter depending on your needs.

Some of the tools included in the book to help you are:

- **Self-test quizzes** to help you decide if you know enough already or if you need to read the chapter in detail.

- **Coaching sessions** enabling you to work through key tasks to cement your learning.

- **Coach's tips** to draw your attention to the key points.

- **Next steps** that review what you've completed during the chapter and link to the next chapter if you prefer to read the book from cover to cover.

- **Takeaways** that will get you into a good habit of reviewing at each stage what you've learned and how you will use this new knowledge.

- **Online resources** including:

  - Templates and spreadsheets to download and complete.

  - Websites where you can research information on companies' performance.

To access the online resources, please follow the link www.TYCoachbooks.com/Finance to the Hodder & Stoughton website. The resources can be accessed from the 'Read extract from book' link on the left hand side of the page.

PART 1
FINANCIAL ACCOUNTING

1

WHAT INFORMATION IS AVAILABLE ON COMPANY PERFORMANCE AND WHERE MIGHT I FIND IT?

 OUTCOMES FROM THIS CHAPTER

- In this chapter we will lay out:
  - What information is only available internally within a company (for the purposes of management control)
  - What is publicly available for all companies
  - What the purposes of financial statements are
  - What kind of information can be gleaned from them

 COACH'S TIP

In the UK, terminology has changed recently for all companies. A summary of new terminology is included at the end of this chapter.

Self-test quiz:

1. What financial information is only available internally within a business?

   -
   -
   -
   -
   -
   -

2. What are the three main financial statements available for all private Limited (Ltd) and Public Limited Companies (plc in UK, or LLC or Inc in the US)?

   -
   -
   -

3. What other accompanying information is available with the published financial statements?

   -
   -
   -
   -

4. Where might you find the published accounts for a Ltd company or plc?

   -
   -

5. What does the Income Statement (also known as a Profit and Loss Account) tell us?

   -

6. What does the Statement of Financial Position (also known as a Balance Sheet) tell us?

   -

7. What does the Statement of Cash Flows tell us?

   -

Suggested solutions

1. What financial information is only available internally within a business? Examples include:

   - Budgets
   - Capital investment proposals
   - Monthly departmental budget vs actual reports
   - Detailed breakdowns of costs by cost type
   - Detailed breakdowns of incomes
   - Internal key performance indicators
   - Etc.

2. What are the three main financial statements available for all Limited (Ltd), Public Limited Companies (plc in UK, or LLC or Inc in the US)?

   - Income Statement (also known as a Profit and Loss Account, or Statement of Operations in the US), including a Statement of Comprehensive Income
   - Statement of Financial Position (also known as a Balance Sheet)
   - Cash Flow Statement

3. What other accompanying information is available with the published financial statements? Examples include:

   - Chairman's statement
   - Directors' report
   - Auditor's report
   - Notes to the accounts
   - Etc.

4. Where might you find the published accounts for a Ltd company or plc?

   - Companies House
   - Their own website

5. What does the Income Statement (also known as a Profit and Loss Account) tell us?

   - What incomes and costs have been incurred and what profit has been made for the period (usually twelve months)

6. What does the Statement of Financial Position (also known as a Balance Sheet) tell us?

   ■ What the company owns or controls vs what the company owes (as a snapshot at the end of the year)

7. What does the Statement of Cash Flows tell us?

   ■ The cash inflows and outflows for a business for a period (usually twelve months), reconciled from profit

COACHING SESSION 1

What financial information would you want to keep track of in your own personal finances?

You would probably want to know:

- What do I earn?
- What do I spend?
- What amount can I save for the things I want to do in the future?
- Will I have enough money to cover any unexpected expenses as they arise?
- What is my house worth?
- What do I owe on my mortgage?
- What other things do I own?
- What do I owe on loans, credit cards, etc.?

These pieces of financial information form the basis of the three main financial statements that all UK Ltd companies and plcs publish every year. In the US, only listed companies (Inc.) are required to publish accounts, so it can be difficult to find financial information for privately owned companies (LLCs – limited liability companies).

 COACH'S TIP

In the UK, small companies only publish abbreviated accounts (a Statement of Financial Position or Balance Sheet).

According to the UK Companies Act 2006, the size of companies is defined as follows:

Small company

If the conditions to be a small company are not met, to be a small company, at least two of the following conditions must be met:

- Annual turnover must be £6.5 million or less.
- The Statement of Financial Position total must be £3.26 million or less.
- The average number of employees must be 50 or fewer.

Medium-sized company

If the conditions to be a small company are not met, to be a medium-sized company at least two of the following conditions must be met:

- Annual turnover must be £25.9 million or less
- The Statement of Financial Position total must be £12.9 million or less.
- The average number of employees must be 250 or fewer.

The **Income Statement** – or *Profit and Loss Account* (or *Statement of Operations* in the US) – lists all the income and costs incurred over the previous period (usually twelve months for published accounts) and shows what profit has been made. This would answer your questions:

■ What do I earn?

■ What do I spend?

■ What amount can I save for the things I want to do in the future?

In addition, there is a **Statement of Comprehensive Income** (which may be included within the Income Statement rather than being shown as a separate statement). This shows changes in equity from non-trading activity, for example actuarial losses on pension schemes, revaluations of property, etc.

The **Statement of Cash Flows** lists all the cash inflows and outflows for the previous period (usually twelve months for published accounts). This would answer your question: 'Will I have enough money to cover any unexpected expenses as they arise?'

The key difference between the Income Statement and the Statement of Cash Flows is that the Income Statement accounts for *transactions as they occur*. A sale is recorded when the goods or services are delivered, the costs are recorded when they are incurred in making the sale (i.e. they are matched to the sale as the sale is recorded). Consequently, sales may be recorded when the customer still owes the money and costs may be recorded when you still owe the supplier the money. By contrast the Statement of Cash Flows shows the real *cash movements* as cash flows into and out of the business as sales income is received and bills are actually paid.

The **Statement of Financial Position** or *Balance Sheet* shows a snapshot at the end of the period of what a company owns or controls vs what it owes. This would answer your questions:

■ What is my house worth?

■ What do I owe on my mortgage?

■ What other things do I own?

■ What do I owe on loans, credit cards, etc.?

COACH'S TIP

In the UK

Larger Limited Companies (Ltd) and Public Limited Companies (plcs) will publish their financial statements on their own websites. Go to their website and look for 'Investor Relations Information' or 'Financial Results', or search for the company name plus 'financial results' using a search engine.

If all else fails, for any Ltd or plc you can buy a copy of their financial accounts from Companies House for a very small fee (currently £1) using http://wck2.companieshouse.gov.uk//wcframe?name=accessCompanyInfo

In the US

Private companies (LLCs) do not have to publish any financial reports.

If the company is publicly traded (Inc.), you have full access to its financial reports. You will probably find them on their own website. Look for 'investor relations' or 'financial reports' or '10K'.

Alternatively input the company name plus 'financial reports' into a search engine and you will be able to access them via the stock markets or commentator sites.

Some of the other information that is published along with the three financial statements for all except *Small Companies* – **see p. 6 for definition** – is:

Information on the business model and strategy (Companies Act 2006; 'a fair review of the company's business').
A market review (Companies Act 2006; 'the main trends and factors likely to affect the future development, performance and position of the company's business').
Information on the financial performance (Companies Act 2006; 'analysis using financial key performance indicators').
Information on different business segments – for example product, market or geographical segments (Companies Act 2006; 'the development and performance of the company's business during the financial year').
Information about the supply chain (Companies Act 2006; 'information about persons with whom the company has contractual or other arrangements which are essential to the business of the company').
Information on risks faced (Companies Act 2006; 'a description of the principal risks and uncertainties facing the company').
Environmental information (Companies Act 2006; 'information about environmental matters', 'information about the company's employees', 'information about social and community issues').
Auditors report. This is a statement by the external auditors to give their opinion of whether the annual report gives a true and fair view of the state of the company's affairs.

Report to the shareholders on how they have applied the UK Corporate Governance Code; for more information see https://www.frc.org.uk/Our-Work/Publications/Corporate-Governance/UK-Corporate-Governance-Code-2014.pdf
Notes to the accounts providing narrative description or detailed breakdowns of items presented in the statements.

Source: Companies Act 2006

 COACH'S TIP

Much of the financial terminology used has changed in recent times and differs by country. A summary of some key terminology follows:

Old UK terminology	New UK terminology	US terminology
Profit and Loss Account	Statement of Income	Statement of Operations; Statement of Income
Balance Sheet	Statement of Financial Position	Balance Sheet; Statement of Financial Position
Debtors	Accounts Receivable; Trade Receivables	Accounts Receivable; Trade Receivables
Creditors	Accounts Payable; Trade Payables	Accounts Payable; Trade Payables
Stock	Inventory	Inventory
Fixed Assets	Non-current Assets	Non-current Assets
Debt	Borrowings	Debt
Long Term Liabilities	Non-current Liabilities	Long Term Liabilities
Depreciation	Depreciation	Amortisation
Shareholder Funds	Equity	Equity

 NEXT STEPS

In this section you have:

• Discovered what financial statements are available for a company and what they tell us.

In the next section we will look in more detail at the Income Statement to see what is included and what we can learn from it.

TAKEAWAYS

This is your opportunity to take stock of what you've learned from this chapter. You might now want to choose other chapters and exercises to focus on, or you can continue to work through the whole book if this better fits your needs.

1. What companies might you be interested in finding out more about?

_____

_____

_____

_____

_____

_____

_____

_____

2. Which financial statements might be of interest to you in looking at these companies?

_____

_____

_____

_____

_____

_____

_____

_____

_____

_____

3. What kind of information do you hope to discover about your chosen companies?

2 HOW DO WE KNOW HOW WELL WE'RE PERFORMING?

 OUTCOMES FROM THIS CHAPTER

- In this chapter we will review the Income Statement – Profit and Loss Account (Statement of Operations in the US) – including:
  - The format and terminology
  - What we can learn about a company's performance from this statement

Self-test quiz:

1. When is a sale a sale (i.e. when can we count a sale in the Income Statement)?
   -

2. What is included in Cost of Sales (COS) or Cost of Goods Sold (COGS)?
   -

3. What does Gross Profit tell us?
   -

4. What is the difference between Cost of Sales (COS) and expenses or overheads?
   -

5. What is operating profit or EBIT?
   -

6. What do EBIT and EBITDA stand for?

    ■

    ■

7. What are accruals?

    ■

8. What are provisions?

    ■

9. What is depreciation?

    ■

10. What happens to profits retained in the business (i.e. those not taken by the owners as dividends)?

    ■

Suggested solutions:

1. When is a sale a sale (i.e. when can we count a sale in the Income Statement)?
   - A sale is a sale when the goods or services are delivered to the customer.

2. What is included in Cost of Sales (COS) or Cost of Goods Sold (COGS)?
   - Direct costs of making the sale; i.e. the costs of the product or service, but not overheads incurred in running the business

3. What does Gross Profit tell us?
   - How much profit has been made on selling products or services after the cost of that product or service has been deducted but before any overhead costs

4. What is the difference between Cost of Sales (COS) and expenses or overheads?
   - COS is the direct cost of selling a product, overheads are indirect costs of running the business

5. What is operating profit or EBIT?
   - Operating profit is the profit made after all direct and indirect costs have been taken into account; it excludes financing costs such as interest and tax

6. What do EBIT and EBITDA stand for?
   - Earnings Before Interest and Tax
   - Earnings Before Interest, Tax, Depreciation and Amortisation

7. What are accruals?
   - Accruals are an estimate of costs incurred in the period for which no invoice has been received

8. What are provisions?
   - Provisions are estimates of costs or liabilities incurred. A provision is very similar to an accrual (in that it is a cost incurred and accounted for on the Income Statement), but there is less certainty over the cost or timing

9. What is depreciation?
   - Spreading the cost of a fixed asset over its useful life

10. What happens to profits retained in the business (i.e. those not taken by the owners as dividends)?
    - Profits retained in the business are added into the equity section of the Statement of Financial Position (Balance Sheet) as a record of where investment money came from

The Income Statement (Profit and Loss Account) is made up as shown here

Income Statement for ABC Ltd for the year ended 31 December 2015

	Note	£
Sales Income	1	500,000
– Cost of Sales	2	(300,000)
= Gross Profit	3	200,000
Expenses	4	
– Selling General and Admin Expenses (Overheads)	5	(20,000)
= EBITDA	6	180,000
– Depreciation and Amortisation	7	10,000
= EBIT (Operating Profit)	8	170,000
– Finance Costs (Interest)	9	5,000
– Tax	10	6,000
= Net Profit	11	159,000
– Dividends	12	10,000
= Retained Profit	13	149,000

1. The Income Statement is about **performance**. A sale is a sale when the goods are delivered, when the company has performed its part of the contract. For ease of administration, because an invoice is usually raised as the goods are despatched, very often the financial IT systems will count the sale when the invoice is raised, but technically the sale actually occurs when the goods are delivered.

   As an example, if you insured a car, irrespective of when you pay the premiums, the insurance company can only claim the sale as they deliver the service. This means that they will count one twelfth of your total premium at the end of each month as they complete their service for that month. If they took the whole sale to the Income Statement when you first bought the insurance policy and then you chose to cancel that policy, they would already have claimed sales that they would have to refund!

2. The Income Statement is also about **matching** the sales made to the cost incurred purely in making that sale.

   Cost of sales is the direct cost of all the goods or services sold. For example, in retail businesses it is only the cost of the product, in manufacturing it is only the cost of the components and the labour cost of assembly, or in a services business it is only the cost of the delivery of the service. This excludes any indirect overheads incurred in running the business.

3. Gross profit is the excess of income over only the direct costs.

COACH'S TIP

We can consider the Income Statement in three separate sections; the first section (up to gross profit) shows us how much money has been made from selling the goods or services. The second section, up to operating profit, shows the profit made after all costs of running the business. The third section, up to net profit, shows the profit made after all costs including financing costs.

4. Expenses (or overheads) are costs incurred in running the business.

5. Examples of overheads are: management salaries, admin costs, utility bills, rent and rates, selling and marketing costs, distribution costs, etc.

COACH'S TIP

Distribution costs and selling costs are normally considered as overheads rather than COS because:

- sales staff are paid a fixed salary irrespective of what they sell and even their commissions are relatively predictable when we budget at the start of the year for the value of sales we plan to make.

- distribution costs (if we have a warehouse, warehouse staff, trucks and delivery drivers) are a relatively fixed cost. If we sell fewer goods, the trucks will still go out to all customers, but with fewer goods on board. Some companies may include distribution in COS; this would be particularly relevant if, for example, distribution were outsourced to a specialist logistics company who charge a fixed rate for each box delivered.

Published accounts tend to show an aggregation of all overheads. Internally, within a business, in the management accounts there will be much more detail included with every cost itemised separately for control purposes.

Because of the *matching concept* we must include in the expenses an estimate of all the costs incurred in the period if the invoice has not yet been received. This is called an accrual. An example of an accrual would be if utility bills are only received quarterly, then each month an estimate of the costs incurred would be accounted for. These accruals would then be reversed out when the invoice is received and accounted for.

For example, consider an expected £300 quarterly utility bill, accrued monthly and reversed every month until the actual bill (£350) arrives in June:

Cost	April	May	June
April utility bill accrual	100		
April accrual reversing		(100)	
May utility bill accrual		200	
May accrual reversing			(200)
June invoice received			350
Total cost included in Income Statement	100	100	150

Additionally there may be provisions in this section. A provision is similar to an accrual, but tends to be for a cost that is likely to occur, but where it is less certain what the full cost will be or when the cost will fall due. For example, a company selling goods under warranty may make a provision for warranty costs to ensure that they are matching costs incurred when the sale is recognised.

A company may make a specific provision if they incur a specific cost. For example, an accidental spillage of toxic materials that requires cleaning up where the full cost is currently uncertain, or a provision for litigation where eventual costs and damages are uncertain.

6. EBITDA stands for Earnings Before Interest, Tax, Depreciation and Amortisation. It is a line of profit commonly used internally within businesses that wish to target internal managers with a profit measure that includes all the costs that are controllable by those managers, but none of the costs that are not controllable (for example, depreciation).

Companies that have invested heavily in infrastructure to support future growth may be incurring such large levels of depreciation that the EBIT is negative (i.e. they are making losses), because they are not yet working to full capacity. In this case, the company may choose to publish EBITDA to show the profits earned at this level, and to show that once they are working (and selling) at full capacity they are likely to make a profit.

Consider the example of a new start-up broadband supplier. By investing heavily in fibre cables, switches and routers, in the early months or years they may make a profit on their sales. However, they are unable to cover the high cost of depreciation. As they sell more services to more customers, this situation will improve. Publishing EBITDA will make it clearer to the readers of accounting information the true state of the business.

In addition, EBITDA is commonly used to value businesses and so a business that is for sale may also publish EBITDA. For full description of business valuation methods, please see *The Business Plan Coach*

7. Depreciation is part of the matching concept; it spreads the cost of a fixed asset over its useful life. If a small business bought a car, then including the full cost of the car in the Income Statement in that same period would adversely affect the profits in that period. This would be unfair as the car will be used for many years in running the business! Consequently companies set policies estimating the useful life of different categories of assets and then spread the cost of these assets over those useful lives.

Consider this example; a business buys a machine for £10,000, which it expects to use for 5 years:

Year	Cost	Depreciation	Net Book Value*
1	10,000	2,000	8,000
2		2,000	6,000
3		2,000	4,000
4		2,000	2,000
5		2,000	0
6		0	0

* Net Book Value (NBV) is the value of the asset included in the Statement of Financial Position (Balance Sheet) at year end. (See chapter 3 for more information on the Balance Sheet.)

As you can see from this example, if the asset is used for longer than the estimated period, then no further depreciation is accounted for in the Income Statement.

COACH'S TIP

Above was an example of straight line depreciation, meaning that the depreciation charge is the same in each year. There are other methods of calculating depreciation. The next most common of which is known as the *reducing balance method*. In this method a fixed percentage of the net book value is charged as depreciation each year. This has the effect of front-end-weighting the depreciation costs. Here's a reducing balance calculation using the same example machine as above:

Year	Cost	% of NBV	Depreciation	Net Book Value
1	10,000	30%	3,000	7,000
2		30%	2,100	4,900
3		30%	1,470	3,430
4		30%	1,029	2,401
5	Assuming the asset is disposed of at the end of year 5, write off the NBV		2,401	0

Amortisation is similar to depreciation. We depreciate a tangible fixed asset (one that we can touch, for example a car) and we amortise an intangible fixed asset (one which we cannot touch, for example software).

8. EBIT stands for Earnings Before Interest and Tax and is also known as Operating Profit. It shows the profit after all business running costs have been taken into account; it excludes financing costs (interest and tax).

COACH'S TIP

The second section of the Income Statement, up to Operating Profit shows the profits made after all the costs of running the operations of the business have been deducted.

9. Finance costs are the interest costs incurred in the period (again, because of the matching concept, we account for costs incurred even if they have not been paid).

10. Tax is the corporation tax on profits. Tax computations are complex because every government in every country has different tax rules. These tax rules are often used to incentivise actions (for example, if a government wishes to incentivise businesses to grow, they may give large tax allowances against capital expenditures).

11. Net profit is the final figure published in the Income Statement and is the 'bottom line' profit earned by the business.

COACH'S TIP

This brings us to the final section of the Income Statement, to net profit, showing the final profit made by the business after all costs.

12. Whilst it is prohibited to show dividends in the Income Statement (as they are not an expense but a distribution of profit), they are shown here to highlight that the net profit of a business is attributable to shareholders who may choose to take some, all or none of the profit as dividends.

13. The retained profits are profits left in the business to fund future growth and are added to the retained earnings (reserves) in the Statement of Financial Position (see chapter 3 for more info).

Discontinued operations: we sometimes see revenues and/or profits separated out between continuing operations and discontinued operations. This is purely to separate the profit or loss made from part of the business sold or closed during the year. It improves the information as it allows you to see what amount of profit or loss will no longer be generated in the future and gives an element of predictive value to the Income Statement.

Now we've reviewed the whole Income Statement and understand all the incomes and costs included in this statement, we can finally review the performance of the business.

MARGINS

Commonly, managers in businesses will be targeted with achieving profit margins. A margin is simply the profit as a percentage of sales turnover.

Below are some margins calculated using our example Income Statement from earlier in this chapter.

Margin	Calculation	Example	Result
Gross Margin is Gross Profit as a percentage of Sales Income	$\frac{\text{Gross Profit}}{\text{Sales Income}} \times 100$	$\frac{200{,}000}{500{,}000} \times 100$	40%
EBITDA Margin is EBITDA as a percentage of Sales Income	$\frac{\text{EBITDA}}{\text{Sales Income}} \times 100$	$\frac{180{,}000}{500{,}000} \times 100$	36%
Operating Margin is EBIT as a percentage of Sales Income	$\frac{\text{EBIT}}{\text{Sales Income}} \times 100$	$\frac{170{,}000}{500{,}000} \times 100$	34%
Net Margin is Net Profit as a percentage of Sales Income	$\frac{\text{Net Profit}}{\text{Sales Income}} \times 100$	$\frac{159{,}000}{500{,}000} \times 100$	32%

It is difficult to say in isolation whether any of these margins are good or bad. It depends very much on the industry as to what margins could be expected. The more competitive the industry is or the more similar the products are (the more likely that competitors will have to compete on price alone), the more likely that all margins will be lower. Whereas highly differentiated products in less competitive markets are likely to give higher margins.

COACH'S TIP

Different industries would have a different business model in terms of their mix of direct and indirect costs.

A telecoms provider would be likely to have a low cost of sales: what does it cost a telecoms provider each time you make a phone call? Consequently their gross margin is likely to be higher. The same telecoms provider however would likely have very high overhead costs: infrastructure, customer services staff, maintenance engineers, etc. so their operating margin would be lower.

A home based consultant would have a high cost of sales (their salary) but very low overheads (working from home) and so their gross margin may be lower, but there would be little difference between their operating margin and their gross margin.

A motor vehicle manufacturer would likely have a relatively high cost of sales (all the costs of the cars) and so their gross margin would be lower than the telecoms provider, but they would also have quite high overheads (admin, research and development, etc.) and so there would be a significant difference between their gross margin and their operating margin.

These different cost structures lead to different business models. Companies with a high gross margin and high overheads will be happy to discount heavily to generate more volume to cover the fixed costs – consider all the adverts you see from the telecoms industry for free evening and weekend calls, free broadband, etc. On the other hand, a company with high cost of sales but low overheads will be less concerned with volume and would not discount heavily to achieve a growth in volume because their key concern is to protect their margins.

It makes sense to compare margins (and indeed all ratios) over time for a company to see if each is getting better or worse, but also to compare with competitors in the same industry to see which companies are performing better or worse.

ONLINE RESOURCE

A downloadable margin calculator is available at:

www.TYCoachbooks.com/Finance

COACHING SESSION 2

You may want to calculate some margins for some companies that you are interested in here. Alternatively, you can download a spreadsheet that will automatically calculate the ratios for you at www.TYCoachbooks.com/Finance

Margin	Calculation	Company 1		Company 2	
		2015	2014	2015	2014
Gross Margin is Gross Profit as a percentage of Sales Income	$\dfrac{\text{Gross Profit}}{\text{Sales Income}} \times 100$				
EBITDA Margin is EBITDA as a percentage of Sales Income	$\dfrac{\text{EBITDA}}{\text{Sales Income}} \times 100$				
Operating Margin is EBIT as a percentage of Sales Income	$\dfrac{\text{EBIT}}{\text{Sales Income}} \times 100$				
Net Margin is Net Profit as a percentage of Sales Income	$\dfrac{\text{Net Profit}}{\text{Sales Income}} \times 100$				

NEXT STEPS

In this section you have:

- Discovered how the Income Statement is made up.

- Understood the accounting treatment of income and costs in the Income Statement.

- Reviewed some margin ratios to establish how to compare performances of different companies.

In the next section we will look in more detail at the Statement of Financial Position to see what is included and what we can learn from it.

 TAKEAWAYS

This is your opportunity to take stock of what you've learned from this chapter. You might now want to choose other chapters and exercises to focus on, or you can continue to work through the whole book if this better fits your needs.

1. Which companies did you review to compare performance?

_____

_____

_____

_____

_____

_____

_____

_____

_____

2. Why did you choose these particular companies – what were you hoping to learn?

_____

_____

_____

_____

_____

_____

_____

_____

_____

_____

3. What reasons can you think of for differences in their margins?

_____

_____

_____

_____

_____

_____

_____

_____

4. How could you check whether your assumptions about the reasons for their different margins are correct?

_____

_____

_____

_____

_____

_____

_____

_____

_____

_____

3

HOW DO WE KNOW WE'LL STILL BE IN BUSINESS IN A YEAR... OR EVEN TOMORROW?

 OUTCOMES FROM THIS CHAPTER

- In this chapter we will review the Statement of Financial Position – or Balance Sheet – including:
  - The format and terminology
  - What we can learn about a company's position from this statement.

Self-test quiz:

1. What does the Statement of Financial Position (Balance Sheet) show us?

    ■

2. What is an Asset?

    ■

3. What is the difference between a Non-Current Asset (Fixed Asset) and a Current Asset?

    ■

4. What is an Intangible Asset?

    ■

5. What is Goodwill?

    ■

6. What is a Liability?

    ■

7. What is the difference between a Non-Current Liability (long term liability) and a Current Liability?

   ■

8. What is Equity?

   ■

9. Why does the Statement of Financial Position balance?

   ■

10. What are the two common layouts of the Statement of Financial Position?

    ■

    ■

11. What is Working Capital?

    ■

    ■

Suggested solutions:

1. What does the Statement of Financial Position (Balance Sheet) show us?

   - The Statement of Financial Position shows what we own or control vs what we owe, or if you prefer, it shows where the money came from and where it is now

2. What is an Asset?

   - An asset is something we own or control

3. What is the difference between a Non-Current Asset (Fixed Asset) and a Current Asset?

   - A non-current asset is intended to be kept for more than one year whereas a current asset will be used up or turned over within one year

4. What is an Intangible Asset?

   - An intangible asset is one that cannot be touched, for example software

5. What is Goodwill?

   - Goodwill is the difference between the price paid to acquire a business and that business's net asset value on the Statement of Financial Position

6. What is a Liability?

   - A liability is something we owe

7. What is the difference between a Non-Current Liability (long term liability) and a Current Liability?

   - A non-current liability is due to be paid after more than one year whereas a current liability is due to be paid within one year

8. What is Equity?

   - The amount of funds contributed by the shareholders plus retained earnings (attributable to shareholders)

9. Why does the Statement of Financial Position balance?

   - The Statement of Financial Position balances due to the accounting equation:

     - Assets = Capital + Liabilities

10. What are the two common layouts of the Balance Sheet?

  - Assets = Capital + Liabilities

Or

  - Assets – Liabilities = Capital

11. What is Working Capital?

- Working capital is the difference between current assets and current liabilities

- Working capital is the amount of money required to keep the business operations running

A Statement of Financial Position (Balance Sheet) is a snapshot at the end of the accounting period that shows where the money came from originally (shareholders' investments and bank loans) and where the money is now (assets). Let's look at a simple Statement of Financial Position of your life:

You decide to buy a house for £500,000, but you don't have £500,000 in cash, so you have to take out a mortgage for £300,000 after paying your deposit of £200,000.

Statement of Financial Position for Reader's Company Ltd as at 31 December 2015

Assets	
House	£500,000
= Total Assets	£500,000
Liabilities	
Mortgage	(£300,000)
= Total Liabilities	(£300,000)
Equity	
Money invested in house	£200,000
= Total Equity	£200,000
= Total Equity + Liabilities	£500,000

This table shows the first option for the layout: Assets = Capital + Liabilities

The following shows an alternative layout: Assets – Liabilities = Capital

Statement of Financial Position for Reader's Company Ltd as at 31 December 2015

Assets	
House	£500,000
= Total Assets	£500,000
Liabilities	
Mortgage	(£300,000)
= Net Assets	£200,000
Equity	
Money invested in house	£200,000
= Total Equity	£200,000

It doesn't really make any difference which layout a company chooses. As you can see, the Statement of Financial Position will balance either way and all the sections, headings and information are the same, just laid out differently.

COACHING SESSION 3

Can you take each item and put it into the correct section of the Statement of Financial Position on the next page?

The items listed in this task are much more complex and detailed than in our last example, but see how many you can identify and categorise. To help you, there are exactly the correct number of spaces (bullet points) in the template that you require, so place the easiest items first then, by process of elimination, you may be able to guess at a few more. The answers are given later with full definitions of each item.

Plant Property & Equipment (PPE)

Provisions

Accounts Receivable (Debtors)

Goodwill

Share Premium

Borrowings (5 year loan)

Borrowings (overdraft)

Cash & Cash Equivalents

Accounts Payable (Creditors)

Investments

Inventory

Called Up Share Capital

Profit and Loss Account Reserves

Statement of Financial Position as at 31 December 2015:

	£
Non-Current Assets	
■	
■	
■	
Total Non-Current Assets	530,000
Current Assets	
■	
■	
■	
Total Current Assets	175,000
Total Assets	705,000
Non-Current Liabilities	
■	
■	
Total Non-Current Liabilities	225,000
Current Liabilities	
■	
■	
Total Current Liabilities	150,000
Total Liabilities	(375,000)
Net Assets	330,000
Equity	
■	
■	
■	
Total Equity	330,000

Here's a full Statement of Financial Position that you can use to check your answers to the last activity. It shows some extra, more complex items in addition to those listed in the last activity. We'll also use this to provide definitions of all the items:

Statement of Financial Position for ABC Ltd as at 31 December:

	Notes	2015 £	2014 £
Non-Current Assets	1		
Plant, Property & Equipment (PPE)	2	200,000	170,000
Investments	3	170,000	120,000
Goodwill	4	160,000	120,000
Total Non-Current Assets		**530,000**	**410,000**
Current Assets	5		
Inventory	6	100,000	50,000
Accounts Receivable	7	50,000	60,000
Cash & Cash Equivalents	8	20,000	10,000
Total Current Assets*		170,000	120,000
Total Assets		**700,000**	**530,000**
Non-Current Liabilities	9		
Borrowings	10	250,000	200,000
Provisions	11	200,000	150,000
Total Non-Current Liabilities		**(450,000)**	**(350,000)**
Current Liabilities	12		
Borrowings	13	150,000	270,000
Accounts Payable	14	119,000	94,000
Tax Liability		6,000	5,000
Accruals	15	6,000	10,000
Total Current Liabilities*		**(300,000)**	**(160,000)**
Total Liabilities		**(750,000)**	**(729,000)**
Net Assets	16	**(50,000)**	**(199,000)**
Equity	17		
Called Up Share Capital	18	100,000	100,000
Share Premium	19	50,000	50,000
Revaluation Surplus	20	70,000	70,000
Retained Earnings (Profit and Loss Account Reserves)	21	(270,000)	(419,000)
Total Equity	22	**(50,000)**	**(199,000)**

* Current Assets – Current Liabilities = Working Capital. See note 23 for Working Capital definition.

The Statement of Financial Position shows where the money came from originally (shareholders' investments and banks) and where the money is now (assets, etc.)

1. *Non-current assets (fixed assets)* – items that the business owns or controls and intends to keep for more than one year. All assets are listed at their original cost less accumulated depreciation (see chapter 2 for more information on depreciation).

2. *Plant, property and equipment* – these are valued at their original cost less accumulated depreciation. There are normally notes to published accounts that will give you more detail on original cost, acquisitions and disposals, accumulated depreciation to date and this year's depreciation charge that would reconcile to the net book value shown on the face of the Statement of Financial Position.

3. *Investments* – the value of shares bought in other companies to be held as an investment. These investments are usually measured at fair value and re-measured each year to reflect an up-to-date value of the investment.

4. *Goodwill* – the difference between the price paid to acquire a business and the net asset value of the business acquired. (See note 16 for net asset value.)

 COACH'S TIP

Let's look at an example to illustrate goodwill: You can see the net asset value of ABC Ltd is £330k from the Statement of Financial Position above. What do you suppose a company wishing to acquire ABC Ltd would have to pay: £330k, more than £330k or less than £330k?

They will likely have to pay more than £330k. They are not just buying the assets of the business, they are also buying the future cash flows (and indeed the person selling the business is losing their income stream, for which they will want to be compensated).

Imagine XYZ Ltd wishes to buy ABC Ltd and, during negotiations, they settle on paying £1m. On the day of acquisition, XYZ will add £330k of net assets into their Statement of Financial Position, but they will pay out £1m of cash from their Statement of Financial Position; their Statement of Financial Position no longer balances! In other words, the net assets are now £670k (£1m–£330k) lower than the total equity.

In order to restore balance, XYZ adds £670k into goodwill (within the non-current assets section) in their Statement of Financial Position; this reflects the difference between the price paid (£1m) and the net asset value of ABC (£330k).

5. *Current assets* – items that the company owns, but they turn over within a year.

6. *Inventory (stock)* – this is an example of a current asset. Inventory can be made up of raw materials, work in progress and finished goods. It reflects all the work to date that hasn't yet been sold. For a services business, there can still be work in progress (WIP); for example in a consultancy business, all the work completed but not invoiced (e.g. salaries of consultants working on partially completed projects) will sit in the WIP until the work is complete, the client is invoiced and the WIP moves to cost of sales in the Income Statement.

7. *Accounts receivable (debtors)* – the total value of all invoices outstanding from customers.

8. *Cash and cash equivalents* – the total value of all cash in hand (in the petty cash tin) and any sums on deposit in instant access current accounts at the bank.

9. *Non-current liabilities* – everything the company owes, but will pay after more than one year.

10. *Borrowings* – the capital sum repayable on all long term loans (e.g. five year loans, mortgages, bonds or debentures, etc.)

11. *Provisions* – a recognition of a cost incurred where the timing of payment or the full cost is uncertain. A non-current provision for example might be a provision for litigation costs or an actuarial estimate of a pension deficit. Here we make the most accurate estimate possible.

12. *Current liabilities* – sums the company owes and will pay within one year.

13. *Borrowings* – the capital sum repayable on shorter term loans, for example where a long term loan is now due within one year, or the value of an overdraft.

14. *Accounts payable (creditors)* – the sum owed to suppliers for goods or services received and invoiced, but not yet paid.

15. *Accruals* – an estimate of the sum owed for goods or services received where the invoice has not yet arrived. It is fairly certain however, there is likely to have been a purchase order detailing the total value.

16. *Net assets* – the sum of all assets less liabilities. Conceptually, if the company sold all its assets to pay off all its liabilities, this would be the amount left over for the shareholders. This is only a very rough figure, because the assets and liabilities listed in the Statement of Financial Position are not valued absolutely accurately at market value. For example, the company's buildings will likely be shown at original cost less depreciation; however, they may have increased in value in the real world.

COACH'S TIP

If the net asset value is very small or negative, this is a strong indicator that there may be solvency issues. If, after selling all the assets, there is not enough to pay all the liabilities, then the company may be insolvent. The definition of insolvency is *'When an organisation can no longer meet its financial obligations with its lender or lenders as debts become due'*.

So the true test would be to look at the liabilities, see when they fall due, then check the Statement of Cash Flows for free cash flow.

17. *Equity* – the amount of the funds contributed by the owners (the shareholders) plus the retained earnings (or losses). The equity section will balance with the net assets.

18. *Called up share capital* – the number of shares issued multiplied by the nominal value of those shares. For example, if, on floating on the stock market, a company sets out to sell 1 million shares at £1 each, the called up share capital will be £1m.

19. *Share premium* – if during the sale of those shares the price increases, or if in the future the company sells more shares at more than the nominal value, then *share premium* reflects the additional sums generated over the £1 nominal value.

20. *Revaluation* – the preferred treatment of property is to value the property at the original cost less accumulated depreciation. An allowed treatment is to revalue the property to market value regularly. If this treatment is applied, then increasing the property value will lead to the Statement of Financial Position not balancing, so in this case, a *revaluation surplus* provides a balancing figure and also alerts the reader to the amount the properties have been revalued by.

21. *Retained earnings* – an accumulation of all profits retained in the business (i.e. not paid out to the shareholders as a dividend) to fund future growth.

22. *Total equity* – should balance with the net asset value.

23. *Working Capital* – a key figure not separated out specifically on the Statement of Financial Position, but nonetheless really important to understand. Working capital is the difference between current assets and current liabilities (it is also known as net current assets). If this is a positive figure, it tells us that in the short term the business has enough cash (or debtors to chase to get cash, or stock to sell to get cash) to pay its bills (creditors, overdraft, etc.) If a business has negative working capital it may be an indicator of liquidity problems.

COACH'S TIP

For example, if this were Tesco's Statement of Financial Position, there would be no problem. Tesco generates cash every day and so, if they do not have enough cash to pay the bills today, they will tomorrow. Furthermore, you could not imagine Tesco's creditors joining together to force Tesco into liquidation!

As another example, if this were a Statement of Financial Position for a company like Amazon, this would reflect a very clever business model where there is little or no stock (with books on 'sale or return'), little or no debtors (customers pay by credit card on ordering) and cash is re-invested in the business very efficiently, leading to very low current assets. However, such a business might pay its creditors relatively slowly, so whilst the working capital figure is negative, this shows a business using creditors' money to fund their business cycle. Again, there would be no concern over their ability to pay creditors as the business generates lots of cash every day.

As a further example, if a manufacturing business had negative working capital, it is likely that this *would* reflect a liquidity problem and supplying such a company might mean slow payments or potentially bad debts.

THE LIQUIDITY RATIO AND THE QUICK RATIO

Typical ratios that can be used to look at liquidity are shown on the table on the next page and calculated for the example Statement of Financial Position for ABC Ltd:

Ratio	Calculation	Example	Result
Liquidity Ratio	Current Assets / Current Liabilities	170,000 / 300,000	0.566
Quick Ratio	(Current Assets – Inventory) / Current Liabilities	70,000 / 300,000	0.233

The point of these ratios is to establish whether the company has enough cash on hand to pay its bills. *Current assets* includes cash, debtors and stock. *Current liabilities* includes creditors and overdrafts. So the **liquidity ratio** shows us whether the company has enough cash, debtors they can collect cash from, or stock they could sell, to pay off their bills.

The liquidity ratio is a good ratio to use to calculate whether a company's stock moves quickly; for example, you would use this ratio for Tesco. If they don't have enough cash right now, their stock will become cash very quickly.

However, if stock moves more slowly, (for example a Christmas tree growing company would only sell its stock in December), it would be unfair to include the stock in the ratio, as it will take a long time to move the stock and turn it into cash. Creditors will not wait that long, so in this case we should use the **quick ratio** and exclude the stock.

A really good result for each of these ratios is 1. Often you will find companies have a ratio of around 0.8, which is probably acceptable. Most accounts payable departments will pay the top 80% of suppliers and juggle the bottom 20%.

COACHING SESSION 4

What three things might concern you when looking at the Statement of Financial Position of ABC Ltd above?

SUGGESTED SOLUTION TO COACHING SESSION 4

What three things might concern you when looking at the Statement of Financial Position of ABC Ltd above?

- The net asset value is negative. This may indicate insolvency; it certainly seems that at these Statement of Financial Position values, selling all the assets would not produce enough money to pay off all the liabilities. In addition, part of the fixed asset value is intangible (the goodwill). This may be a further concern: what is the underlying value of the acquisition? If the acquisition isn't working out well and returning as much profit as anticipated, the situation may be worse than it looks! (If the acquired business is not producing as much profit as anticipated, then the business should write down or 'impair' the goodwill shown to reflect the price they would pay if buying the business today.)

- The working capital is negative, this may be an indication of liquidity problems; however, we would need to know more about the business and its industry to be sure.

- The business seems to have been making losses, possibly for many years. The retained earnings are negative, indicating an accumulation of losses. The most recent Income Statement (in the previous chapter) shows a profit, and you can see here that the retained losses are reducing, so maybe the business has been able to turn around their run of losses recently.

QQ COACHING SESSION 5

You may want to calculate some ratios for some companies that you are interested in here:

Alternatively, you can download a spreadsheet that will automatically calculate the ratios for you at www.TYCoachbooks.com/Finance

Ratio	Calculation	Company 1		Company 2	
		2015	2014	2015	2014
Liquidity Ratio	Current Assets / Current Liabilities				
Quick Ratio	(Current Assets – Inventory) / Current Liabilities				

WHAT IS THE DIFFERENCE BETWEEN PROFIT AND CASH? WORKING CAPITAL IN MORE DETAIL

Imagine you have a manufacturing business where on average:

- raw materials are held in stock for four weeks prior to production
- production takes two weeks
- finished goods are held for six weeks
- debtors take sixty days (eight weeks) to pay

Here's the same example shown in a timeline:

Weeks																			
1	2	3	4	5	6	7	8	9	10	11	12	13	14	15	16	17	18	19	20

Raw Mats | Prod'n | Finished Goods | Debtors

goods received

production starts

prod'n complete

invoice raised, goods delivered

customer pays

In this example, if we paid for everything up front, then cash paid out would be tied up in the working capital cycle for twenty weeks (or five months) before the money was received from the customer.

However, it's very unlikely that we would pay for everything up front. Credit terms are usually agreed with suppliers:

- raw materials' creditors have given us credit terms of sixty days (eight weeks)
- production staff are paid monthly
- overheads are paid monthly

Let's add this information to our timeline:

1	2	3	4	5	6	7	8	9	10	11	12	13	14	15	16	17	18	19	20
Raw Mats				Prod'n			Finished Goods					Debtors							
Raw Mats Creditors							← cash tied up in raw mats - 3 mths →												
				Prod'n Staff			← cash tied up in labour - 3 mths →												
Overheads			← cash tied up in overheads - 4 mths →																

The key time frames to note here are the amounts of time the cash is tied up in the working capital cycle until the money is received from the customer.

Another key point to note is that many people think that as long as your creditor days (the time taken to pay suppliers) is longer than your debtor days (the time taken to collect cash from the customer) then your cash will be positive. This is clearly not true because this ignores the amount of time that the stock is held! Here in our example, the debtor and creditor days are the same, but cash is tied up in stock for three months because of the time taken in stock holding and production.

We can further calculate how much money we would need to fund our working capital cycle.

Whilst this simple illustrated time line only looks at a single iteration through the working capital cycle, we know that we don't run one working capital cycle from start to finish and then start the next one. Instead we receive materials in every day, we start production every day, we finish goods and send them to the warehouse every day, we make deliveries every day and we receive payment in from customers every day. Likewise we're making payments to creditors every day.

Think about it: if we overlay our timeline with many more timelines starting each day, at any point in time, on any day of the year, we'd have about three months' worth of money tied up in raw materials, about three months' worth of money tied up in labour costs and about four months' worth of money tied up in overheads.

If you know your budget for a year, we can calculate how much money is required to fund the working capital cycle. Let's say that our annual budget is:

Raw materials £1,000k
Labour   £ 800k
Overheads   £ 600k

If we plan to spend £1,000k on raw materials in a year and we know that at any moment in time we have about three months' worth of money tied up in raw materials, then we need only multiply £1,000k by three months out of twelve, i.e. £1,000k × 3 / 12 = £250k.

If we plan to spend £800k on labour in a year and we know that at any time we have about three months' worth of money tied up in labour costs, then £800k × 3 / 12 = £200k.

Finally, if we plan to spend £600k on overheads and at any time we have four months' worth of money tied up in overheads, then £600k × 4 / 12 = £200k.

In total we need £650k cash to keep the working capital cycle running.

Finally, anything that can be done to improve the working capital cycle will reduce the investment required.

For example, if raw materials are delivered in closer to 'just in time', if production is made faster and more efficient, if goods are delivered out to customers more quickly and so held in stock for less time, if customers can be persuaded to pay more quickly and if we can negotiate longer payment terms with suppliers:

Weeks																			
1	2	3	4	5	6	7	8	9	10	11	12	13	14	15	16	17	18	19	20

Raw Mats | Prod'n | Finished Goods | Debtors

Raw Mats Creditors

If we were able to reduce the working capital cycle as suggested in the timeline above, from raw material delivery to payment from the customer in ten weeks, yet our terms with our suppliers is now twelve weeks, we'd be receiving the money from the customer before we had to pay our raw materials supplier! We'd be funding our business using the creditors' money, just like the Amazon example above which would hugely improve cash management and give more breathing space if customers are slow to pay.

We can measure the working capital for a business using the following ratios and example calculations for ABC Ltd are shown here:

(You will need to look for the sales and cost of sales figures in the Income Statement shown in chapter 2.)

Ratio	Calculation	Example	Result
Stock days	$\dfrac{\text{Inventory}}{\text{Cost of Sales}} \times 365$	$\dfrac{100,000}{300,000} \times 365$	122
Debtor days	$\dfrac{\text{Accounts receivable}}{\text{Sales}} \times 365$	$\dfrac{50,000}{500,000} \times 365$	37
Creditor days	$\dfrac{\text{Accounts payable}}{\text{Cost of Sales}} \times 365$	$\dfrac{125,000}{300,000} \times 365$	152

It is difficult to determine what good working capital ratios are without making a comparison to companies from the same industry. Comparing this ratio to different industries will not provide any insights at all. For example, a house builder may buy land and hold onto it for many years waiting for planning permission; consequently house builders may have average stock days of 500–600! Compare this to a grocery store that may have stock days of 7–14.

Likewise, most industries have fairly standard payment terms for customers and suppliers, so comparison of debtor days and creditor days to the standard terms in the industry would be more useful than viewing the figures in isolation.

COACHING SESSION 6

You may want to calculate some working capital ratios for some companies that you are interested in here:

Alternatively, you can download a spreadsheet that will automatically calculate the ratios for you at www.TYCoachbooks.com/Finance

Ratio	Calculation	Company 1		Company 2	
		2015	2014	2015	2014
Stock days	$\dfrac{\text{Inventory}}{\text{Cost of Sales}} \times 365$				
Debtor days	$\dfrac{\text{Accounts receivable}}{\text{Sales}} \times 365$				
Creditor days	$\dfrac{\text{Accounts payable}}{\text{Cost of Sales}} \times 365$				

WHAT'S THE DIFFERENCE BETWEEN CAPEX AND OPEX? WHY DO I NEED TO KNOW?

Capital Expenditure (CapEx) is the acquisition of non-current assets (or fixed assets): things we own or control and mean to keep or use for more than one year.

Operating Expenditure (OpEx) – also known as revenue expenditure or expenses – are day to day running costs that would be included in the Income Statement.

⍥⍥ COACHING SESSION 7

Looking at this list of items for a small training company, tick which item would be CapEx and which would be Opex.

	Item	CapEx	OpEx
1	Computer equipment		
2	Salaries of trainers		
3	Projector		
4	Repairs to the projector		
5	Stock of training materials and books		
6	Annual licence with a data provider		
7	Leasehold of training rooms		
8	Leasehold improvements to training rooms		
9	Rent of training rooms		
10	Legal fees to recoup doubtful debts		
11	Website to promote the business		
12	Cost of trainer taking an MBA course at local university		
13	Purchase of a new flipchart stand		

⍥⍥ SUGGESTED SOLUTION TO COACHING SESSION 7

	Item	CapEx	OpEx	Comments
1	Computer equipment	✓		Computer equipment is usually CapEx. However, some organisations will have an internal rule to exclude computer equipment from CapEx; this may be on the basis that often computer equipment becomes obsolete so quickly.
2	Salaries of trainers		✓	This is OpEx and would show in cost of sales.
3	Projector	✓		This is a non-current asset on the Statement of Financial Position.

(*Continued*)

4	Repairs to the projector		✓	Anything that maintains the expected speed, efficiency, life or productivity of an asset is simply maintenance or repairs, and therefore OpEx. However, anything that improves the speed, efficiency, life or productivity of an asset may be an upgrade and therefore a CapEx item in its own right.
5	Stock of training materials and books		✓	This would be an item of inventory on the Statement of Financial Position in the current assets section and would go through the cost of sales in the Income Statement as the items are used on courses.
6	Annual licence with a data provider		✓	As an annual licence, it will expire within one year, so it will be OpEx and shown in the expenses section of the Income Statement.
7	Leasehold of training rooms	✓		Purchase of a long leasehold is CapEx.
8	Leasehold improvements to training rooms	✓		Leasehold improvements are CapEx too, the business will benefit from these improvements for many years.
9	Rent of training rooms		✓	This is a day to day running cost shown in the Income Statement expenses section.
10	Legal fees to recoup doubtful debts		✓	Day to day running cost shown in the Income Statement expenses.
11	Website to promote the business	✓		As an intangible item, providing the business can show that this is an asset that generates income for the business, then it is CapEx.
12	Cost of trainer taking an MBA course at local university		✓	This is simply a day to day running cost. The business does not own the trainer, so cannot capitalise this item, as the trainer may leave and take their knowledge with them!
13	Purchase of a new flipchart stand	✓		Whilst this is an item that may be kept for more than one year, the price of it is very low. Each business will have a capital expenditure threshold; a value above which items are capitalised, but below which items are written off through the Income Statement. Businesses set their own capital threshold, but a common figure would be £1,000. This is part of the underlying concept of materiality; if the value is small, the readers of the accounts would not be able to tell the difference whether the item was capitalised or not, so it may as well be written off. However, many flipchart stands bought at the same time would be capitalised!

In business, operational managers usually have the ability to manage their own OpEx budgets at their own discretion; however, CapEx items are usually controlled differently. Often business managers will need to produce a CapEx request, a proposal showing the costs and benefits of the expenditure, to invest in non-current assets because of the size and scale of this investment. At the very least, the expenditure will give rise to many future years of depreciation that will need to be accounted for, hence requiring a specific proposal.

Sometimes managers may prefer to capitalise purchases (include them in the non-current assets section of the Statement of Financial Position), or to expense them in the Income Statement. For example, a manager with a very tight budget may prefer to capitalise purchases in order that the cost is spread over a number of periods. Alternatively, if the CapEx proposal and authorisation process is bureaucratic, they may prefer to manage the cost through their own budget.

If a company is cash rich, the manager may prefer to purchase assets with cash, paying up front and possibly receiving a discount, in which case they may prefer to capitalise the cost. Alternatively, if they have little cash, they may choose to lease an asset and spread the cash payments over many years. Lease costs are OpEx.

Additionally, if a company is trying to show a high return on assets (ROA), they may prefer to expense items (write them off through the Income Statement), rather than capitalise them, to keep the assets figure low, although the additional expenses would also impact the return part of this ratio. However, some companies may be trying to show growth in investment so would prefer to capitalise!

If you are trying to sell high value products to a customer, you may wish to structure the deal differently depending on the finances of the customer. You could:

- Give away the product but charge a high monthly maintenance fee, or lease a product rather than sell it outright if the customer is short of cash or prefers not to capitalise.

- Charge a one-off high fee and keep maintenance costs to a minimum if the customer is cash rich and prefers to capitalise items.

There are other considerations for a customer:

- If they have a very high cost of sales, in order to improve their gross margin (see chapter 2) they may be willing to increase their overheads to pay for a new system, process or solution to drive down the cost of sales.

- If they have a very high level of overheads and are trying to show that they have firm control of costs, they may be willing to capitalise a large expenditure that saves overheads (bearing in mind that the depreciation of the capitalised item would need to be lower than the overhead saved!)

The same considerations are valid if you are trying to purchase high value items, depending on your own company finances.

WHY DOES IT MATTER HOW WE'RE FUNDED?

A business may be funded by shareholders (equity) or by loans (debt). Gearing is a measure of how a business is funded, it looks at the proportion of long term funding that comes from loans.

$$\frac{\text{Non-Current Borrowings}}{\text{(Total Equity + Non-Current Borrowings)}} \times 100$$

Loans are inherently riskier than equity. With a loan, the capital sum must be repaid, whereas called up share capital is a non-distributable reserve, which means that it is not paid back.

In addition, a business funded heavily by loans will have a large fixed cost of interest to pay in each period, so in a sales downturn, where profits are reduced, the business may struggle to pay the interest costs. However, a business funded entirely by equity in the same situation will simply not pay a dividend.

Shareholders will normally prefer the business to have some gearing. Imagine a situation where you invest £100 in a business. Let's say the business makes a £6 profit in the first year, that's a 6% return for you.

Now imagine the same business (having more growth opportunities than you can fund with your £100) goes to the bank and borrows £100 as well. Chances are that the business will not make double the profit, after all, it will need to pay the interest costs. However, it may make £2 more profit. That is now an 8% return for you at no extra investment from you!

A common level of gearing for most plcs is 30% where non-current loans are 30% of the total capital employed (non-current loans + total equity). We usually find that banks charge lower interest rates for companies with gearing up to 30%, but as the gearing rises, so do the interest rates. Many banks will not extend loans to companies with high gearing and will also put covenants on any loans to ensure the gearing doesn't exceed their target value.

A business with very cyclical or seasonal sales would be better served with a lower gearing, because they would have to consider how to cover interest costs in a low sales (and therefore low cash generation) period.

There are many types of funding and financial instruments available. The table on the next page describes each option, the benefits and drawbacks and the impact on control:

Funding option	Description	Benefits	Drawbacks	Impact on control
Grants	This is an attractive option as many government agencies and charities may be able to fund a wide range of business activities, from start-up, funded apprenticeship schemes, research and development, training, etc.	It's free funding or subsidies for activities that you would have had to pay for anyway.	There may be complicated application and review processes. It may take time to gain the funding. The conditions of grants often include you having to match the funding from the grant, so you can only receive half of the full funds you need. There may be 'claw back' clauses if you don't fulfil your conditions.	In some cases, there may be conditions placed on the grant, affecting your plans.
Overdraft	An overdraft is a short term facility agreed with your bank to temporarily spend more than the funds available in your account. A limit to the overdraft is agreed with the bank.	You only pay interest on the amount you use, as you use it. Therefore, it's much more flexible and cheaper than if you take out a loan to cover a l your needs for a longer period of time. It's quick and easy to agree with the bank. There are no fees for paying it off (unlike with a fixed term loan if you choose to pay it off early).	The interest rates and charges for using your overdraft facility can be higher than the interest charged on a fixed term loan. You will be charged more if you go over your overdraft limit. You will probably have a one-off fee as you go over plus your interest will increase too. The bank can recall the overdraft at any time for any (or no) reason. There will usually be a charge if you want to extend your overdraft.	There is no loss of control or decision making.

(Continued)

Funding option	Description	Benefits	Drawbacks	Impact on control
Bank Loans	Bank loans or loans from public sources can be for almost any time frame with any level of interest. It's important to establish your funding needs early to give you time to shop around and to negotiate the best rates for you. Interest may be fixed, so it won't change over the life of the loan, giving you confidence and security. Interest may be variable, so it will change as the Bank of England changes its base rate, or as the lender's costs change.	The good thing about a loan is that it will have a fixed term and the bank cannot demand repayment early (unlike an overdraft). The lender has no control over your business activities and decision making nor will they take a share of your profits (unlike with shareholders).	There may be conditions on a loan, known as loan covenants, where the lender sets certain conditions, for example a cap on gearing, or target profitability levels. If these loan covenants are breached, the lender could demand repayment early. There may be charges if you want to repay the loan early. Loans may need to be secured against an asset. If you struggle to make the interest payments, the lender may not be sympathetic and take the asset. If the value of the asset doesn't cover the outstanding loan value, the lender may still pursue you for additional payments. If the interest rate charged is variable, you may struggle to plan and manage your finances.	There is little impact on control of your business and decision making unless you breach your loan covenants. Read the terms of any loan carefully and seek legal advice before committing to any contracts, to ensure you understand any consequences in case of early repayment, breach of loan covenants or failure to make the interest payments.

Leasing (operating leases)	Here, instead of taking out a loan to buy an asset, you could instead lease the asset.	The leasing company has to maintain and repair the asset if it breaks down. Lease costs are fixed each month, giving you confidence in financial planning. At the end of the lease period you can give the asset back, buy it for a small fee, or replace the asset with a new lease. This is better for cash flow, spreading the costs, than buying outright with cash.	If you don't keep up payments you will lose the asset. You can only take out an operating lease on an asset, for example when buying a new machine, so it won't cover working capital requirements (i.e. you can't lease stock). You might not be able to get out of the contract early if your needs change. It is usually more expensive than owning the asset over the whole life of that asset.	No loss of control or decision making.
Sell shares in your business	Here, the investor takes ownership of a share of the company, receives part of the profits and may want to influence the business plan and business decisions.	Bringing in an investor with specific business skills may help you with ideas, contacts and business skills that you don't possess. There are no interest payments to be made. Dividend payments are voted on by all the shareholders so, depending on what share of the business you have sold, if you retain the controlling share, you will have ultimate control over whether a dividend is paid or not.	Finding investors and contracting with them can be difficult, time consuming and expensive. You lose: ■ some control of the business and decision making ■ some of the profits ■ some of the final sale value if the business is sold later. This is only an option if you are a limited company (private limited Ltd, or public limited plc) as sole traders and partnerships can't sell shares. (See chapter 5 for more information on different legal forms of companies).	Some control and decision making is lost depending on the size of the share of the business sold.

(Continued)

Funding option	Description	Benefits	Drawbacks	Impact on control
Private Equity	Private equity finance is provided for a stake in the business. Usually only companies with potential for high growth are attractive to private equity investors. Although, they are normally established businesses requiring some additional funding for growth, or needing specific expertise or to improve efficiencies. The private equity firm raises funds from insurance companies and pension funds, individuals, etc. The private equity firm normally takes part in the management of the business funded. Private equity firms will normally have an exit strategy, to grow the business for a short period of a few years, then sell out for a profit.	You don't just gain funding, but also business acumen and any particular expertise needed to grow the business or to improve efficiencies.	As with selling shares, you lose a great deal of control and decision making.	As above with 'Shareholders' a loss in control and decision making, depending on the size of the stake sold.
Venture Capital	Venture capital firms are very similar to private equity firms, the only real difference is that they normally specialise in investing in new start-ups where there is no track record and cash needs are great.	As above	As above	As above

| Factoring | With factoring, you sell your debtors (invoices owed to you by customers) to a factoring company who pay you a portion of the value, then they collect the money from the customer directly for themselves. | You receive cash up front as soon as you invoice instead of having to wait for customers to pay. | Depending on the factoring company you use you could receive only 75–85% of the money.

Customers may lose confidence and source alternative suppliers if they think you have cash flow problems, unless you tell them up front that this is your policy for all customers. | No loss of control or decision making. However, if customers don't pay, you have no involvement or understanding of the process the factoring company may use to collect. If their processes or their mistakes upset your customers, you may lose them. |

(Continued)

Financial Instrument	Description	Benefits	Drawbacks
Hedging	Hedging is a method of reducing risk; for example, if you are buying or selling products overseas then currency exchange rate fluctuations may impact your profitability. Hedging is a method of offsetting the effect of exchange rate fluctuations by making a financial transaction opposite to your product transaction. For example if you have a contract to sell £100k of products to the US in three months' time (assuming the current exchange rate is £1 to $1), you expect to earn $100k in three months, which is the equivalent of £100k. What if in the meantime the exchange rate changes to £1 = $1.50? In this example you will still receive $100k but it will be worth only £66k. At the time of signing the product sale contract, the company could make a hedging deal to sell $100k for £100k in three months' time.	Hedging stops any losses being made on contracts to supply goods or services in the future in the instance that exchange rates change for the worse.	No benefits can be made on contracts to buy or sell products or services overseas if the exchange rate improves. Accounting for hedges is complicated and can mean that losses or gains need to be recognised in profit, causing volatility.

| Interest Rate Swaps | An interest rate swap is a method that companies use to exchange interest rate payments with each other.

One company may want to receive a payment with a variable interest rate, whilst the other wants to limit future risk by receiving a fixed-rate payment instead.

A gain for one party will be a loss to the other.

Here's an example: ABC Company and XYZ Company enter into one-year interest rate swap with a nominal value of £1m. ABC offers XYZ a fixed annual rate of 5% in exchange for a rate of LIBOR plus 2%, since both believe that LIBOR will be about 3%. At the end of the year, ABC will pay XYZ £50k (5% of £1 million). If the LIBOR rate is 4%, XYZ then will have to pay ABC £60k (6% of £1 million), i.e. LIBOR 4% + 2% premium. | Companies can choose to make fixed or variable payments in order to take advantage of improving interest rates, or to reduce the risk of increasing interest rates. | An interest rate swap is a zero sum game, so one party to the transaction will gain but the other will lose.

Accounting implications as above. |

→ NEXT STEPS

In this section you have:

- Understood the layout, terminology and purpose of the Statement of Financial Position, and discovered the warning signs of solvency and liquidity.

- Understood the importance of working capital and how to manage it.

- Calculated some key ratios.

- Understood the rules surrounding capital expenditure vs operating expenditure and why individuals or companies may prefer one or the other when purchasing high value items.

- Understood how companies are funded.

In the next section we will look in more detail at the Statement of Cash Flows to see what is included and what we can learn from it.

TAKEAWAYS

This is your opportunity to take stock of what you've learned from this chapter. You might now want to choose other chapters and exercises to focus on, or you can continue to work through the whole book if this better fits your needs.

1. Which companies did you review to compare gearing, liquidity and working capital management?

_____

_____

_____

_____

_____

_____

_____

_____

2. Why did you choose these particular companies – what were you hoping to learn?

_____

_____

_____

_____

_____

_____

_____

_____

_____

3. What reasons can you think of for differences in their results?

_____

_____

_____

_____

_____

_____

_____

_____

_____

4. How could you check whether your assumptions about the reasons for their different results are correct?

_____

_____

_____

_____

_____

_____

_____

_____

_____

_____

4 WHAT IS THE REAL CASH POSITION?

✔ OUTCOMES FROM THIS CHAPTER

- In this chapter we will review the Statement of Cash Flows, including:
  - The format and terminology
  - What we can learn about a company's cash position from this statement.

Self-test quiz:

1. The Statement of Cash Flows reconciles which two figures?

   -
   -

2. What are the three main sections of the Statement of Cash Flows?

   -
   -
   -

3. Give examples of cash flows arising from operating activities.

   -
   -
   -

4. Give examples of cash flows arising from investing activities.

   -
   -
   -

5. Give examples of cash flows arising from financing activities.

   ■

   ■

   ■

6. Other than cash, what is included in a Statement of Cash Flows? Give an example.

   ■

Suggested solutions:

1. The Statement of Cash Flows reconciles which two figures?
   - Operating profit
   - Net cash flow

2. What are the three main sections of the Statement of Cash Flows?
   - Operating activities
   - Investing activities
   - Financing activities

3. Give examples of cash flows arising from operating activities.
   - Sales income
   - Cost of goods or services
   - Tax payments or refunds

4. Give examples of cash flows arising from investing activities.
   - Proceeds on disposal of non-current assets, cash outflow on capital expenditure
   - Payments or receipts to acquire or sell equity or debt of other companies
   - Payments and receipts related to loans or advances to other companies

5. Give examples of cash flows arising from financing activities.
   - Repayment of borrowings
   - Payments or receipts on selling or redeeming the company's shares
   - Cash receipts from issuing loans or bonds, etc.

6. Other than cash, what is included in a Statement of Cash Flows? Give an example.
   - Cash equivalents – These are highly liquid investments, such as money held in a current account

The Statement of Cash Flows is a tricky statement to understand. Depending on the accounting standards complied with there are two allowed formats:

- The first is simply a list of cash transactions; sales income and expenditure. Whilst this format is actually quite intuitive to understand, being very similar to your bank statement, it is not commonly used.

- The second is the most common format, which we will examine here.

This format starts from the operating profit figure from the Income Statement and then makes adjustments to turn this from profit to cash. This may seem a complicated way of presenting the information; however, most computer accounting systems are set up to account on an accruals basis (when costs are incurred as opposed to when the cash moves).

If you consider the operating profit line on the Income Statement, everything up until that point may bear no relation to real cash movements.

RECONCILING PROFIT AND CASH

- Sales are counted when the goods or services are delivered, not when the customer pays, so there would be a difference between profit and cash.

- Cost of Sales is the costs of goods *sold*. More may have been bought and held in stock, plus the cost of sales may not have been paid for yet – they may have been bought on credit. So again there would be a difference between profit and cash.

- Overheads may include accruals (for costs incurred but not yet paid for) and provisions (provisions are a recognition of a cost incurred, but not yet completely quantifiable – consider if an employee has an accident on your site and takes the company to court for compensation. The accident has happened, but at this stage you can only estimate the compensation. You would have to account for the cost incurred in the Income Statement, as an estimate. This would be called a provision). Accruals and provisions, by definition, have not been paid and therefore reflect a difference between profit and cash.

- Depreciation is listed in the overheads, but it is not a cash item. It's another difference between profit and cash.

- The operating profit line in the Income Statement is above interest and tax, so any interest or tax paid would not have been taken into account yet, so again there is a difference between profit and cash.

- Dividends are not shown on the published Income Statement, but dividends are paid out of net profits. Again, these are not reflected in the operating profit. This is yet another difference between profit and cash.

- There are a number of items that don't make it onto the Income Statement at all. For example, non-current assets purchased, loans taken out or paid off, etc. These again have to be taken account of to get from profit to cash.

In this note we'll explain how the Statement of Cash Flows is compiled in order to help you understand the layout of the Statement of Cash Flows that you need to analyse.

Here are the steps required to move from operating profit to cash:

1. Start with operating profit (EBIT) from the Income Statement.

2. Add back depreciation. This was not a cash item. We're trying to move from profit to cash, so we will add back all non-cash items that have been charged against profit.

3. If there is an increase in accounts receivable from last year's Statement of Financial Position to this year's, the company must have collected less money from customers. These sales have been counted in the operating profit, so we must deduct this to get to a cash figure (and vice versa).

4. If there is an increase in accounts payable from last year's Statement of Financial Position to this year's, then the company must have paid fewer creditors than is accounted for in the Cost of Sales. It would be a positive adjustment to move from profit to cash (and vice versa).

5. If inventory has increased from last year's Statement of Financial Position to this year's then more stock has been bought, which represents a cash outflow and a negative adjustment to the operating profit (and vice versa).

6. Finally, make negative adjustments to the operating profit for any interest, tax, dividends paid, fixed assets acquired, loans paid, etc. Make positive adjustments to operating profit for any loans taken out, shares sold, etc.

⨀⨀ COACHING SESSION 8

Let's try it out. From the Income Statement and Statement of Financial Position for ABC Company Ltd, try to compile the Statement of Cash Flows below:

(The same Income Statement and Statement of Financial Position for ABC Ltd are replicated below for you to refer to)

Statement of Cash Flows for ABC Company Ltd for the year ended 31/12/2015

	£
Operating profit	
Add back depreciation and amortisation	
Less increase in inventory	
Add decrease in accounts receivable	
Add increase in accounts payable	
Add back increase in provisions	
Add back increase in accruals	
= Operating cash flow	
Less interest paid	
Less dividends paid	
Less tax paid	
Plus loans taken out	
Less payments to acquire non-current assets	
Plus overdraft paid off	
= Net cash flow	

Income Statement for ABC Ltd for the year ended 31 December 2015

	Note	£
Sales Income	1	500,000
− Cost of Sales	2	(300,000)
= Gross Profit	3	200,000
Expenses	4	
− Selling General and Admin Expenses (overheads)	5	(20.000)
= EBITDA	6	180,000
− Depreciation and Amortisation	7	10,000
= EBIT (operating profit)	8	170,000
− Finance Costs (interest)	9	5,000
− Tax	10	6,000
= Net Profit	11	159,000
− Dividends	12	10,000
= Retained Profit	13	149,000

Statement of Financial Position for ABC Ltd as at 31 December:

	Notes	2015 £	2014 £
Non-Current Assets	1		
Plant, Property & Equipment (PPE)	2	200,000	170,000
Investments	3	170,000	120,000
Goodwill	4	160,000	120,000
Total Non-Current Assets		530,000	410,000
Current Assets	5		
Inventory	6	100,000	50,000
Accounts Receivable	7	50,000	60,000
Cash & Cash Equivalents	8	20,000	10,000
Total Current Assets*		170,000	120,000
Total Assets		700,000	530,000
Non-Current Liabilities	9		
Borrowings	10	250,000	200,000
Provisions	11	200,000	150,000
Total Non-Current Liabilities		(450,000)	(350,000)
Current Liabilities	12		
Borrowings	13	150,000	270,000
Accounts Payable	14	119,000	94,000
Tax Liability		6,000	5,000
Accruals	15	25,000	10,000
Total Current Liabilities*		(300,000)	(379,000)
Total Liabilities		(750,000)	(729,000)
Net Assets	16	(50,000)	(199,000)
Equity	17		
Called Up Share Capital	18	100,000	100,000
Share Premium	19	50,000	50,000
Revaluation Surplus	20	70,000	70,000
Retained Earnings (Profit and Loss Account Reserves)	21	(270,000)	(419,000)
Total Equity	22	(50,000)	(199,000)

* Current Assets – Current Liabilities = Working Capital.

😧😧 SUGGESTED SOLUTION TO COACHING SESSION 8

	£	Notes
Operating profit	170,000	Straight from the Income Statement (IS).
Add back depreciation and amortisation	10,000	Straight from the IS, depreciation is not a cash item so add it back to the profit to get closer to real cash flow.
Less increase in inventory	(50,000)	Compare the two stock figures for 2014 and 2015 on the Statement of Financial Position in the current assets. Inventory has been bought, so cash must have flowed out of the business.
Add decrease in accounts receivable	10,000	Compare the two accounts receivable figures for 2014 and 2015 on the Statement of Financial Position in the current assets. If receivables decreased, more cash was collected than is recognised in the operating profit.
Add increase in accounts payable	25,000	Compare the two accounts payable figures for 2014 and 2015 on the Statement of Financial Position in the current assets. If payables increased, then fewer suppliers were paid so less cash was paid out than recognised in the operating profit.
Add back increase in provisions	50,000	Compare the provisions figures for 2014 and 2015 – provisions are not a cash item, so accounting for them within the operating profit reduced the profit, but not the cash!
Add back increase in accruals	15,000	Compare the accruals figures for 2014 and 2015 – accruals are not a cash item, so accounting for them within the operating profit reduced the profit but not the cash!
= Operating cash flow	230,000	Total up the figures to this point.
Less interest paid (finance costs)	(5,000)	The interest is listed on the IS, but we should check that it was actually paid! If it had not been paid it would be listed in the Statement of Financial Position as a liability. In this case it was not, so it must have been paid.
Less dividends paid	(10,000)	The dividends proposed are listed on the IS, again we need to check that these were actually paid in the year.

Less tax paid	(5,000)	The tax due is listed on the IS. However, we're trying to find out what cash was paid out in 2015. The tax was calculated after the year end after the IS was compiled, so could not have been paid in 2015. Check the Statement of Financial Position and you can see this year's tax is listed as a liability. So they must have paid last year's tax during this year.
Plus loans taken out	50,000	Compare the loan figures for 2015 and 2014 on the Statement of Financial Position in the non-current liabilities.
Less payments to acquire non-current assets	(130,000)	If you thought the assets bought were worth £120k (the difference between 2014 and 2015's non-current assets), you have not taken into account the depreciation. If the company had bought no assets, the £410k for 2014 would have depreciated by £10k to £400k in 2015. The actual figure for 2015 is £530k, therefore £130k (£530k–£400k) of assets were bought.
Less overdraft paid off	(120,000)	Compare the overdraft figures for 2015 and 2014 on the Statement of Financial Position in the current liabilities.
= Net cash flow	10,000	Total up the column to this point.

We can confirm that this is correct because the difference between cash on the Statement of Financial Position for 2014 and 2015 is £10k.

You may be wondering why we bothered with a Statement of Cash Flows if it was clear how cash had moved from the Statement of Financial Position. The answer is that we can see much more from the Statement of Cash Flows than by just looking at the Income Statement and Statement of Financial Position alone.

Analysing the Statement of Cash Flows

The way to analyse this Statement of Cash Flows is to firstly look at whether all the profits were turned to cash.

COACH'S TIP

It is really important that we can turn our profits to cash. If we only focus on the Income Statement and see that the business is profitable, but we ignore the Statement of Cash Flows and so do not notice that we are not collecting cash from our customers, we might go bust, despite our profits! The danger comes if we're paying our suppliers promptly but spending more than necessary on holding huge amounts of stock.

Not forgetting that depreciation, provisions and accruals are not cash items, we hope to see from the previous cash flow statement on pages 63–64, operating profit (170k) + depreciation (10k) + provisions (£50k) + accruals (15k) = £245k should equal operating cash flow (which was actually £230k). This is not far off, so we're not too worried. The company has paid fewer payables (efficient), taken on more inventory (not very efficient) and has collected fewer of its receivables outstanding (not very efficient), which explains the difference.

Moving to the next section of the Statement of Cash Flows, we see that the company has paid interest, tax and a very small dividend; there's not much to comment on there. Whilst each has had an impact on the cash flow, these are transactions that are necessary to do business.

The company paid off a large portion of the overdraftwhich, given their positive operating cash generation, is probably a good idea.

They took out long-term borrowings, which possibly went towards the purchase of a non-current asset. Most of the cash generated went into buying non-current assets, which is a productive thing. So all in all, most of the cash was used wisely in this year.

One thing to check is what types of assets were bought. If you look at a real Statement of Financial Position, there will always be a note number against the non-current assets. Look up the note and you will likely see assets grouped into categories and you'll see the original costs, acquisitions, disposals and depreciation. If money was spent on buildings or machines, or any kind of productive asset, this is a good thing as it provides more capacity for more profits in the future.

If the assets bought were fixtures and fittings (e.g. a refurbishment, or worse still, a fountain in reception) then there will be no return on this investment and the money is lost. You can't tell exactly what type of building, machine or fixtures are bought, the note doesn't give that much detail – but it does provide you with some questions to ask.

→ NEXT STEPS

In this section you have:

- Understood the Statement of Cash Flows and how to analyse it.

In the next section we will look at how we can analyse accounts for companies in very different industries.

TAKEAWAYS

This is your opportunity to take stock of what you've learned from this chapter. You might now want to choose other chapters and exercises to focus on, or you can continue to work through the whole book if this better fits your needs.

1. Which companies did you review to compare cash flows?

_____

_____

_____

_____

_____

_____

_____

_____

2. How did the cash flow compare to the profitability?

_____

_____

_____

_____

_____

_____

_____

_____

_____

3. What were the key uses of cash in the business (for example, investment or paying off loans)?

_____

_____

_____

_____

_____

_____

_____

_____

4. How do you feel about the generation and use of cash in the businesses reviewed?

_____

_____

_____

_____

_____

_____

_____

_____

_____

_____

5

I NEED TO FEEL CONFIDENT LOOKING AT ACCOUNTS FOR BUSINESSES IN VERY DIFFERENT INDUSTRIES

 OUTCOMES FROM THIS CHAPTER

- In this chapter we will look at:
  - A method for determining what we expect to see in the accounts for different companies in different industries.
  - All the financial statements for some example companies.

Self-test quiz:

1. What are the features you'd see in the accounts or ratios of a national grocery store that might distinguish it from any other business?

   -
   -

2. What key item of cost would a pharmaceutical company incur, much more than companies in other industries?

   -

3. What do you imagine the inventory days figure would be for a construction (house building) company?

   -

4. Which of these companies is likely to have the longest trade accounts receivable days?

   - Tesco
   - Amazon   ☐
   - Sky   ☐

5. What item would you find on the Statement of Financial Position for a football club that you wouldn't find for any other business?

   ■

6. What kinds of ratios would you calculate to establish the performance, efficiency and risk of a business?

   ■

   ■

   ■

Suggested solutions:

1. What are the features you'd see in the accounts or ratios of a national grocery store that might distinguish it from any other business?

   a. Low margins

   b. Rapid stock turnover

2. What key item of cost would a pharmaceutical company incur, much more than companies in other industries?

   a. Research and Development (R&D)

3. What do you imagine the inventory days figure would be for a construction (house builder) company?

   a. Up to 600

4. Which of these companies is likely to have the longest trade accounts receivable days?

   a. Tesco   ☐

   b. Amazon   ☐

   c. Sky   ☑

5. What item would you find on the Statement of Financial Position for a football club that you wouldn't find for any other business?

   a. Players' contracts

6. What kinds of ratios would you calculate to establish the performance, efficiency and risk of a business?

   a. Profitability (margins, ROCE, etc.)

   b. Inventory days, receivables days, payables days

   c. Gearing

Now that we've looked at all the financial statements we can start to analyse the performance of the business.

In order to do this we must first look at the big picture and determine what we expect to see in the accounts of the business to be analysed so that we know what kinds of ratios we are expecting. To do this we will perform a SCIRE analysis (Sector, Company, Information available, Ratios and Evaluation):

Section	Questions to ask / information to find	Analysis of the situation
Sector To start with, simply brainstorm everything that you know about the industry, ask people who might know about the industry and do some internet research	Is it growing or is it in decline?	If the industry is growing, providers may be able to charge higher prices. At least they're unlikely to be in direct price competition, so gross margins may be higher.
	Is it very competitive with many commodity providers, or is it very differentiated?	In a commodity market, price competition will be fierce leading to lower margins.
	Is there much consolidation in the industry (companies acquiring each other)?	If there is a lot of consolidation, maybe there is over-capacity in the market that may adversely affect margins. Also, with many acquisitions, investments will be high, so any return on investment ratios may be depressed.
	What is the business model (where are most of the costs in the industry – in cost of sales or in overheads)?	If more of the cost is in cost of sales, it will be important to the competitors to keep prices high and maintain margins. If overheads are high and cost of sales low, competitors will be keen to discount to gain more customers to cover the overheads.
	Have there been any one-off events affecting the industry?	Any events – such as an ash cloud, a terrorist event, or a major change in price in a key raw material – will affect margins.
Company To start with, simply brainstorm everything that you know about the company, ask people who might know and do some internet research	Is the business a high end provider with a differentiated product or mainly competing on cost leadership?	This will have a big impact on the margins. Companies can charge more for differentiated products, which will lead to higher margins. Cost leaders may choose to charge the same price as competitors and maintain high margins, or they may pass cost savings onto customers, to compete on price, lowering their margins.

	Are they an innovative company launching new products?	If so, there will be high investments in R&D. How are they funding this? Is gearing high?
	What kind of assets does this company hold?	If high fixed assets are required, where did they get the funding? Is gearing high? Is a lack of capital constraining their growth? If a large stock holding is necessary, how is this affecting their cash management and liquidity ratios?
	Is the business growing or in decline?	If growing, how are they funding this? Is gearing high? Are there high investments in marketing and capital investments? In the short term, these will reduce the operating margin and Return on Investment (ROI) ratios. If sales are falling, how is the company controlling or reducing their fixed costs to keep profits stable?
Information Available Read the chairman's statement and directors' reports, look at the business's website	Review the company strategy and commentary about the market.	Does it line up with what you thought in the previous two sections?
Ratios	See next section for a thorough exploration of ratios.	
Evaluate	Once you've completed all the ratios, compile all the information you've gathered and determine: ■ Is the company doing the right things given the state of the market? ■ Do the ratios fit with your estimates? ■ How does each company compare to its competitors? ■ Do the written statements and ratios line up?	

Let's put this altogether and review the accounts of some companies in the broadcast media industry: the BBC, ITV and Sky.

COACHING SESSION 9

Firstly, consider what you already know about the broadcast media industry and the three companies we're reviewing. What impact would the information you've identified have on the financial results? Which ratios will be affected? Make some notes below.

Section	Questions	Your analysis of the situation
Sector To start with, simply brainstorm everything that you know about the industry, ask people who might have some knowledge of the industry and do some internet research	Is it growing or is it in decline?	
	Is it very competitive with many commodity providers, or is it very differentiated?	
	Is there much consolidation in the industry (companies acquiring each other)?	
	What is the business model (where are most of the costs in the industry – in cost of sales or in overheads)?	
	Have there been any one-off events affecting the industry?	
	Any other information?	

Now, what do you know about the three companies we are considering?

		BBC	ITV	Sky
Company To start with, simply brainstorm everything that you know about the companies, ask people who might have some knowledge and do some internet research	Is the business a high end provider with a differentiated product or mainly competing on cost leadership?			
	Are they an innovative company launching new products?			
	What kind of assets does this company hold?			
	Is the business growing or in decline?			
Information Available Read the chairman's statement and directors' reports, look at the business's website	Review the company strategy and commentary about the market; does it line up with what you thought in the previous two sections?			

SUGGESTED SOLUTION TO COACHING SESSION 9

Be aware that the comments in the Sector and Company sections are entirely the opinions of the author and are not to be taken as facts.

Section	Questions	Our opinions
Sector To start with, simply brainstorm everything that you know about the industry, ask people who might have some knowledge of the industry and do some internet research	Is it growing or is it in decline?	The market for services is probably growing, at least in line with the increase in population. With the recent economic downturn, chances are that people will be staying in more. Because of the relatively new flexibility to view programmes on-demand using a number of platforms, there should be opportunities for growth. However, growth in advertising spend with broadcast media is likely to be flat or possibly in decline with the growth of internet and social media channels for advertising. Therefore we'd be expecting a small increase in revenues.
	Is it very competitive with many commodity providers, or is it very differentiated?	We'd expect to see a very competitive industry. Despite the proliferation of channels, the small number of providers each hold a large market share. Points of differentiation may be: ■ On-demand platforms ■ Added value services (websites, weather apps, sports betting, etc.) ■ Quality of news reporting nationally and depth of local of news ■ Popularity of entertainment shows ■ Licence for provision of sports coverage ■ The latest movies Given the competition, margins are likely to not be improving particularly over the two years of comparison. Given the investment in new technologies and costs of licences, ROCE (Return on Capital Employed) is likely to be squeezed.

	Is there much consolidation in the industry (companies acquiring each other)?	In the past few years there have been acquisitions and Competition Commission reviews of the impact on competition. Acquisitions may result in lower ROCEs in the early years after acquisition because of the costs of integration.
	What is the business model (where are most of the costs in the industry – in cost of sales or in overheads)?	In this industy, the Cost of Sales (programming) will be a large proportion of total costs. However, overheads (technology, marketing, etc.) could also be large. We can expect a fairly even split between programming costs and overheads.
	Any other information?	Efficiency is likely to be key to all providers given the post-2008 economic downturn, for the publicly funded competitors this will be a constant objective. We'll want to carefully review the expenses ratio to see how the companies are controlling their overheads. Sky focus on customer retention as well as organic growth through provision of extra services to existing customers. Through growth, we'd expect to see efficiencies in overheads, but Sky also have a large home communications business (broadband and telecoms), which is a lower margin business, so it will be interesting to see how this mix affects their ratios as the communications business grows. ITV have published transformation plans to diversify their business to be less reliant on advertising revenues. We'd need to discover more about what the plans involve. Typically, any kind of restructuring can lead to exceptional items or provisions for restructuring costs. EBIT and ROCE would be affected if this were the case.

(The following information is the view of the author prior to reviewing the accounts and is intended only to give the reader a view of what is important to look at in the accounts.)

Company		BBC	ITV	Sky
To start with, simply brainstorm everything that you know about the companies, ask people who might have some knowledge and do some internet research	Is the business a high end provider with a differentiated product or mainly competing on cost leadership?	The BBC stands for very high production standards, quality news coverage, public interest and education provision, and an unbiased approach. We would expect fairly stable investment. Because the BBC is publicly funded, a growth in income does not mean the same as it would for the other competitors. As there are no shareholders there is no share capital so gearing will appear high. However, this is not a problem, just a feature of not-for-profit organisations.	ITV are a large commercial free-to-air family of channels. We'd hope to see some cost leadership. However, with reductions in advertising revenues in the past, they focused on finding new sources of revenue, which may cost more to establish in the early years. Advertising revenues seem to have increased recently, so it's possible we'll see some revenue growth. Recent acquisitions may mean that their revenue growth is inflated, it would be difficult to determine how much of their revenue growth is sustainable.	Sky tend to differentiate through a broad range of value added services and products, and have focused on winning sports contracts, the latest movie releases and box sets. Whilst the cost of this content is likely to be high, it enables Sky to grow its customer base and therefore subscription income, so their margins may still be healthy in comparison to the other competitors.
	Are they an innovative company launching new products?	The BBC invests heavily in value added services, were quick to launch iPlayer and is looking at internet-only channels. Being publicly funded, there may be a requirement to invest the licence fee in new technologies.	With their transformation strategy, ITV focus on more paid-for, platforms, so that investments provide a return (unlike the BBC); for example, their subscription ITV player app on iOS.	Sky have invested heavily in the past in being quick to launch Sky+, HD, NOW TV and, more recently, SkyGo. Sky also have a large home communications business (broadband, etc.) so are not a like for like comparison to the other companies.

	Any companies that invest most heavily in technologies that become obsolete quickly would need to achieve high ROCE percentages. For example, if technology becomes obsolete in three years on average, then a ROCE of around 30% would mean they could use profits to replace assets every three years. None of these businesses have technologies that become obsolete quickly, so ROCEs below 30% will be acceptable.
What kind of assets does this company hold?	Depending on whether the company buys in licences there may be a great deal of intangible assets on the balance sheet. If they mainly produce their own content, this would not be capitalised. If the companies produce a lot of their own programming, there will be a great deal of inventory (part-completed work in progress). Large advertising revenues may lead to longer receivables days than licence fee income or subscription income, which should be fairly certain in their timings.
Is the business growing or in decline?	Probably has the lowest growth in income in the sector due to public funding and the pressure to keep costs down. / Probably the largest growth in revenues, assuming that their turnaround plans are successful and given their acquisitions. / Probably reasonable growth, given the retention and organic growth strategy combined with the focus on growth in products and services.
Any other information?	These competitors are likely to buy in a varying amount of their programming from independent production companies and studios, and to pay out for sports licences – possibly reducing margins where content is bought in – as they are paying for the suppliers' mark-up rather than paying just their own production costs. The mix of own produced vs bought in will be important. The BBC is more likely to produce more of its own content, being the public service broadcaster for the UK. ITV's production vs bought-in content will likely be around 50:50. Sky will buy in content from Hollywood Studios and the Premier Football League, and major production companies – for example HBO – but are increasing investment in UK commissioned programming. Furthermore, for very popular programmes, prices will be higher. Purchase of content will lead potentially to higher payables days.

Information Available				
Read the chairman's statement and directors' reports, look at the business's website	Review the company strategy and commentary about the market; does it line up with what you thought in the previous two sections?	To paraphrase, the BBC is prioritising valuable content and looking for efficiencies, some coming from restructuring and simplified governance. Almost a quarter of the BBC's revenues was 'other income', which may be commercial activities, for example selling DVDs and content overseas, etc.	To paraphrase, ITV are focusing on four key strategies: 1. Efficiency 2. Maximise share 3. New revenue streams 4. International content. It is maintaining its leading position in advertising. Growth is coming from some acquisitions as wel as new markets and platforms. Quality creative content is key.	To paraphrase, Sky are growing in three main areas; 1. Paid-for TV where there are still 13m households in the UK and Ireland not paying for TV 2. There is strong growth in demand for new 'pay light' services (NOW TV, etc.) 3. The transactional market (digital rather than DVDs) with the Sky Store brand

RATIOS

We have already calculated a number of ratios as part of chapters 2 and 3, but now let's put them all together and review them in detail. Ratios are a really useful way of comparing financial results of different companies.

The companies you want to analyse will be different sizes with different turnover and different levels of investment. By calculating ratios, you can compare like with like.

We will look at a number of different ratios:

- Profitability on sales

    - How profitable are the companies you are evaluating?

    - How much money do they make on selling goods?

    - What do they spend on running the business (the overheads)?

    - What net profit do they make after all costs?

- Return on investment

    - What profits do they make as a percentage of the investment made?

- Measures of efficiency

    - How well do they manage their working capital and therefore their cash? Poor cash management is one of the biggest reasons for business failure. A review of how much other businesses in the industry invest in working capital and how they manage their cash flow will be helpful for you to compare against. In many industries, credit terms with customers are fairly standard across the industry, the same is true of credit terms with suppliers. In addition, most businesses in the industry will have similar stock holdings in terms of days. They will all be trying to manage their stock as efficiently as they can.

- Liquidity ratios

    - How well do competitors in this industry manage their cash flow?

    - Is cash tight? Do they have enough cash to pay payables on time? If not, do they have suitable overdraft facilities to cover this?

- Risk ratios

    - The gearing ratio will show you how much the business had to borrow (compared to money invested by the owners) to start-up, run and grow. The greater the gearing percentage (i.e. the more that is borrowed compared to owners' investments), the higher interest rates are likely to be. As a rough guide, 30% gearing is seen as quite reasonable but anything much higher than 30% could lead to high interest rates and difficulties in gaining more loan funding.

Ratio	Calculation	Comments
Profitability on Sales		
Gross Margin	$\dfrac{\text{Gross Profit}}{\text{Annual Sales}} \times 100$	Profit made on selling goods or services before overheads are paid. Needs to be compared to competitors to determine if gross margin percentage is good.
Expenses	$\dfrac{\text{Expenses}}{\text{Annual Sales}} \times 100$	If a company is growing its sales, its fixed overheads should stay relatively stable so the ratio should go down. Sometimes during growth managers 'take their eye off the cost control ball', this ratio will highlight this issue. If a company's sales are in decline, you'd look for them to take action to reduce overheads and keep the ratio stable.
Operating Profit Margin	$\dfrac{\text{Operating Profit (EBIT)}}{\text{Annual Sales}} \times 100$	Comparison to competitors is required to determine whether the ratio is good.
Net Profit Margin	$\dfrac{\text{Net Profit}}{\text{Annual Sales}} \times 100$	Comparison to competitors is required to determine whether the ratio is good.
Return on Investment (ROI)		
Return on Capital Employed (ROCE)	$\dfrac{\text{Operating Profit (EBIT)}}{(\text{Total Equity} + \text{Non-Current Borrowings})} \times 100$	Must be more than the cost of capital (cost of interest and dividends as a percentage of total capital employed) plus a reasonable return to the shareholders.
Measures of Efficiency		
Stock Days	$\dfrac{\text{Stock}}{\text{Cost of Sales}} \times 365$	The average number of days that stock is held for. Shorter is more efficient: ties up less cash. If stock days are long, check the liquidity.
Debtor Days	$\dfrac{\text{Debtors}}{\text{Sales Revenue}} \times 365$	Average number of days it takes to collect cash from customers.

Creditor Days	$\dfrac{\text{Creditors}}{\text{Cost of Sales}} \times 365$	Average number of days it takes to pay suppliers.
Liquidity Ratios		
Current Ratio	$\dfrac{\text{Current Assets}}{\text{Current Liabilities}}$	A ratio of close to 1 or more is good, as it means the company can pay all its bills. Take into account the business model. If the business generates lots of cash, the current ratio could be lower than 1 and still be viable.
Quick Ratio	$\dfrac{(\text{Current Assets} - \text{Inventory})}{\text{Current Liabilities}}$	If stock days are long, it's not realistic to include stock in the current assets, it would take too long to sell them and get the cash in to pay the bills that are due now. The solution to this ratio, as with the current ratio, should be close to 1 or more.
Risk		
Gearing	$\dfrac{\text{Non-Current Borrowings}}{(\text{Total Equity} + \text{Non-Current Borrowings})} \times 100$	Gearing is a measure of risk. A company 100% funded by debt is risky as it will have to pay a high fixed cost of interest. Any small drop in sales and profits will make it difficult to pay the interest. However, some gearing is desirable, to leverage the owners' investment. Around 30% gearing is usually seen as reasonable by banks. Greater gearing will probably lead to higher interest rates being charged by banks.
Interest Cover	$\dfrac{\text{Operating Profit}}{\text{Interest (finance costs)}}$	If gearing is high, calculate the interest cover to determine whether the interest is affordable. The higher this ratio, the more times over the company can pay its interest costs from operating profits.

Here are the financial statements for the BBC , ITV and Sky.

As you'll notice, the year-end dates for each company are different, so the comparison years chosen show the greatest overlap possible. However, it does mean that the ITV accounts are the oldest.

The ratios are already calculated for you for these companies in the section straight after these accounts. You may want to work back using the ratios table above and the accounts that follow here to ensure you can find the right number and calculate the same ratio results for yourself.

BBC FINANCIAL STATEMENTS

Consolidated income statement

	Note	2014 £m	Restated* 2013 £m
Licence fee income	A1	3,726.1	3,656.2
Other income	A1	1,339.9	1,446.1
Total income	A1	5,066.0	5,102.3
Operating costs excluding specific items		(4,721.9)	(4,808.1)
Exceptional impairment of tangible and intangible assets	B1	–	(51.7)
Restructuring costs	C3	(16.5)	(43.7)
Total operating costs	A1	(4,738.4)	(4,903.5)
Group operating surplus		327.6	198.8
Gain on sale and termination of operations	E3	4.1	23.3
Other gains and losses	E4	(16.5)	–
Gain on disposal of fixed assets	D3	–	87.2
Share of results of associates and joint ventures	E4	22.7	23.0
Financing income	F9	14.6	10.2
Financing costs	F9	(163.6)	(146.5)
Net financing costs	F9	(149.0)	(136.3)
Surplus before taxation		188.9	196.0
Taxation	G2.1	(35.1)	(38.7)
Surplus for the year		153.8	157.3
Attributable to:			
BBC		153.8	156.4
Non-controlling interests		–	0.9
Surplus for the year		153.8	157.3

*IAS 19 (revised) Employee benefits has been adopted for 2014 and accordingly the 2013 comparatives have been restated (see page 78).

As the BBC Group is run for the public benefit, the surplus arising does not represent a 'profit' that can be distributed, but is retained for future investment.

Consolidated balance sheet

	Note	At 31 March 2014 £m	At 31 March 2013 (restated)* £m	At 1 April 2012 (restated)* £m
Non-current assets				
Intangible assets (including goodwill)	E1	233.2	159.5	289.4
Property, plant and equipment	D1	1,305.6	1,370.3	1,451.8
Interests in associates and joint ventures	E4	13.0	31.5	31.3
Other receivables	F6.1	25.8	80.3	30.6
Assets available for trading	D2	108.9	121.5	100.9
Derivative financial instruments	G4.2	6.0	4.9	2.3
Deferred tax assets	G2.4	9.5	15.1	13.4
		1,702.0	1,783.1	1,919.7
Current assets				
Programme-related assets and other inventories	B5	730.5	645.6	691.7
Trade and other receivables	F6.2	988.7	931.3	875.2
Assets classified as held for sale	G1	–	9.9	90.9
Derivative financial instruments	G4.2	12.9	4.0	3.4
Cash and cash equivalents	F1	526.1	575.2	407.3
		2,258.2	2,166.0	2,068.5
Current liabilities				
Trade and other payables	F7.1	(959.7)	(1,033.2)	(1,118.3)
Borrowings	F3.1	(7.7)	(27.0)	(36.8)
Provisions	F8	(53.3)	(66.0)	(86.1)
Derivative financial instruments	G4.2	(2.8)	(10.1)	(4.2)
Current tax liabilities		(14.8)	(12.5)	(13.1)
		(1,038.3)	(1,148.8)	(1,258.5)
Non-current liabilities				
Other payables	F7.2	(15.2)	(18.4)	(73.6)
Borrowings	F3.2	(1,008.2)	(1,043.1)	(1,052.9)
Provisions	F8	(56.8)	(71.5)	(68.0)
Derivative financial instruments	G4.2	(14.4)	(10.6)	(5.9)
Deferred tax liabilities	G2.4	(3.1)	(0.7)	(6.0)
Pension liabilities	C7.1	(1,515.7)	(1,615.8)	(1,078.6)
		(2,613.4)	(2,760.1)	(2,285.0)
Net assets		308.5	40.2	444.7
Attributable to the BBC:				
Operating reserve		226.9	(51.9)	309.2
Available for sale reserve		91.6	107.3	95.2
Hedging reserve		5.4	(7.3)	1.0
Translation reserve		(15.4)	(7.9)	32.1
		308.5	40.2	437.5
Non-controlling interests		–	–	7.2
Total capital and reserves		308.5	40.2	444.7

* The Group has presented a third balance sheet as at 1 April 2012 because the retrospective changes to IAS 19 (revised) *Employee benefits* have a material impact on the information presented in the statement.

The financial statements were approved by the Executive Board on 19 June 2014 and signed on its behalf by:

Tony Hall
Director-General

Anne Bulford
Managing Director Finance and Operations

Notes to the accounts

F. Managing funding (including future costs) continued

F6.2 Trade and other receivables due within one year

	2014 £m	2013 £m
Trade receivables	217.9	224.3
Licence fee receivables	407.3	404.9
Amounts owed by associates and joint ventures	19.4	27.7
VAT recoverable	43.2	46.4
Other receivables	103.5	64.1
Prepayments and other assets	197.4	163.9
Total	988.7	931.3

Included in the BBC Group's trade and other receivables at 31 March 2014 are balances of £42.9million (2013: £43.9million) which are past due at the reporting date but not impaired. The aged analysis of these balances is as follows:

Trade receivables past due but not impaired	2014 £m	2013 £m
Up to 3 months	31.5	33.1
3 to 6 months	4.6	8.3
Over 6 months	6.8	2.5
	42.9	43.9

In determining the recoverability (likelihood of receiving payment) of a trade receivable the Group considers any change in the credit quality of the trade receivable from the date credit was initially granted up to the reporting date. Trade receivables are provided for based on estimated irrecoverable amounts, determined by reference to past default experience of the counterparty and an analysis of the counterparty's financial situation.

There are no significant impairment provisions relating to balances of any individual debtor. Amounts charged to the impairment provision are written off when there is no expectation of recovery. Subsequent recoveries of amounts previously written off are credited to the income statement. The impairment provision stands at £5.5million at 31 March 2014 (2013: £11.8million).

The movement in the allowance for doubtful debts is set out below:

	2014 £m	2013 £m
Balance at the beginning of the year	11.8	5.5
Impairment losses recognised	5.5	8.0
Amounts written off as uncollectable	(10.8)	(0.6)
Amounts recovered during the year	(1.0)	(1.0)
Exchange differences on revaluation	–	(0.1)
Balance at the end of the year	5.5	11.8

No significant amount has been provided for items that are not yet due for payment.

Notes to the accounts (*Continued*)

F7 Trade and other payables
This note details the amounts payable to third parties by the BBC Group.

F7.1 Trade and other payables due within one year

	Note	2014 £m	2013 £m
Trade and employment related payables		424.6	444.2
Amounts owed to associates and joint ventures		5.9	5.9
Other taxation and social security		26.3	26.5
Other payables		19.9	35.6
Accruals and deferred income (including licence fee payables)		422.7	442.7
Cash balance payable to DCMS	B6	7.3	17.9
Licence savings stamp deposits and direct debit instalments		53.0	60.4
Total		**959.7**	1,033.2

F7.2 Other payables due after more than one year

	2014 £m	2013 £m
Other payables	15.2	18.4
Total	**15.2**	18.4

It is the BBC's policy to comply with the Better Payment Practice Code in relation to the payment of suppliers, provided that the supplier is complying with their contracted terms and conditions. The BBC monitors compliance against the terms of this code. Payments for programme acquisitions are made in accordance with contractual terms. The Group's number of days outstanding in respect of other trade payables at 31 March 2014 was 23 days (2013: 25 days).

Notes to the accounts

B3 UK PSB Group expenditure

B3.1 UK PSB Group expenditure by service

2014 Service	Content £m	Distribution £m	Infrastructure/ support £m	Other items £m	Total £m
BBC One	1,023.7	51.0	236.4	–	1,311.1
BBC Two	400.0	28.8	93.0	–	521.8
BBC Three	81.0	5.9	22.4	–	109.3
BBC Four	48.9	4.3	12.7	–	65.9
CBBC	76.1	5.5	19.3	–	100.9
CBeebies	28.7	4.6	9.3	–	42.6
BBC ALBA	5.2	1.3	1.5	–	8.0
BBC News Channel*	48.7	8.0	9.5	–	66.2
BBC Parliament	1.7	7.2	1.5	–	10.4
BBC Red Button	13.5	21.9	4.1	–	39.5
Television	**1,727.5**	**138.5**	**409.7**	**–**	**2,275.7**
BBC Radio 1	40.2	5.8	6.8	–	52.8
BBC Radio 2	47.8	5.7	7.3	–	60.8
BBC Radio 3	40.8	5.8	10.1	–	56.7
BBC Radio 4	91.8	9.0	19.8	–	120.6
BBC Radio 5 Live	49.2	5.7	11.6	–	66.5
BBC Radio 5 Live Sports Extra	2.4	1.4	1.4	–	5.2
BBC 1Xtra	5.6	1.6	2.6	–	9.8
BBC 6Music	7.9	1.6	2.5	–	12.0
BBC 4 Extra	4.1	1.6	1.7	–	7.4
BBC Asian Network	6.6	1.8	2.4	–	10.8
BBC Local Radio	115.4	10.8	23.4	–	149.6
BBC Radio Scotland	22.6	3.2	6.4	–	32.2
BBC Radio nan Gàidhael	3.8	1.4	1.0	–	6.2
BBC Radio Wales	13.4	1.4	3.8	–	18.6
BBC Radio Cymru	11.7	1.6	3.5	–	16.8
BBC Radio Ulster/BBC Radio Foyle	17.4	1.3	4.9	–	23.6
Radio	**480.7**	**59.7**	**109.2**	**–**	**649.6**
BBC Online**	**106.5**	**18.8**	**49.1**	**–**	**174.4**
Spend regulated by service licence	2,314.7	217.0	568.0	–	3,099.7
Licence fee collection costs	–	–	–	102.1	102.1
Orchestras and performing groups	22.8	–	5.1	–	27.9
S4C	23.4	–	5.7	76.3	105.4
Development spend	45.2	–	10.0	–	55.2
BBC Monitoring	–	–	–	7.2	7.2
UK PSB Group pension deficit reduction payment	–	–	–	48.6	48.6
Costs incurred to generate intra-group income	–	–	–	169.3	169.3
Costs incurred to generate third party income	–	–	–	60.6	60.6
Other content related spent	**91.4**	**–**	**20.8**	**464.1**	**576.3**
Restructuring costs	–	–	–	9.6	9.6
Total UK PSB Group content expenditure	**2,406.1**	**217.0**	**588.8**	**473.7**	**3,685.6**
Digital switchover (DSHS Limited)	–	–	–	7.2	7.2
Local TV***	–	–	–	16.0	16.0
Broadband rollout***	–	–	–	150.0	150.0
Total UK PSB Group expenditure	**2,406.1**	**217.0**	**588.8**	**646.9**	**3,858.8**
Lease reclassification****	–	–	–	(81.0)	(81.0)
UK PSB Group expenditure	**2,406.1**	**217.0**	**588.8**	**565.9**	**3,777.8**

Notes to the accounts

B. How the BBC spends the funds continued

B3.1 UK PSB Group expenditure by service continued

2013 Service	Content £m	Distribution £m	Infrastructure/ support £m	Other items £m	Total £m
BBC One	1,129.2	52.9	281.1	–	1,463.2
BBC Two	404.8	31.7	106.6	–	543.1
BBC Three	89.7	4.6	27.4	–	121.7
BBC Four	50.0	4.2	16.0	–	70.2
CBBC	81.6	4.0	23.1	–	108.7
CBeebies	28.9	4.5	9.6	–	43.0
BBC ALBA	4.9	1.5	1.4	–	7.8
BBC News Channel*	45.2	7.5	8.8	–	61.5
BBC Parliament	1.9	7.2	1.4	–	10.5
BBC Red Button	15.6	22.3	3.9	–	41.8
Television	**1,851.8**	**140.4**	**479.3**	**–**	**2,471.5**
BBC Radio 1	40.7	5.4	8.1	–	54.2
BBC Radio 2	47.8	5.3	9.0	–	62.1
BBC Radio 3	38.3	5.3	10.7	–	54.3
BBC Radio 4	91.1	9.8	21.2	–	122.1
BBC Radio 5 Live	55.0	6.8	14.2	–	76.0
BBC Radio 5 Live Sports Extra	2.7	1.4	1.5	–	5.6
BBC 1Xtra	7.5	1.5	2.8	–	11.8
BBC 6Music	7.4	1.5	2.6	–	11.5
BBC 4 Extra	4.0	1.5	1.7	–	7.2
BBC Asian Network	8.3	1.7	3.0	–	13.0
BBC Local Radio	114.7	9.9	27.9	–	152.5
BBC Radio Scotland	23.2	3.2	6.3	–	32.7
BBC Radio nan Gàidhael	3.8	1.4	1.1	–	6.3
BBC Radio Wales	13.9	1.2	3.7	–	18.8
BBC Radio Cymru	12.5	1.6	3.5	–	17.6
BBC Radio Ulster/BBC Radio Foyle	17.0	2.1	4.7	–	23.8
Radio	**487.9**	**59.6**	**122.0**	**–**	**669.5**
BBC Online**	**103.0**	**21.8**	**51.8**	**–**	**176.6**
Spend regulated by service licence	2,442.7	221.8	653.1	–	3,317.6
Licence fee collection costs	–	–	–	111.1	111.1
Orchestras and performing groups	23.4	–	5.8	–	29.2
S4C	23.6	–	6.4	–	30.0
Development spend	40.4	–	10.1	–	50.5
UK PSB Group pension deficit reduction payment	–	–	–	48.6	48.6
Costs incurred to generate intra-group income	–	–	–	164.8	164.8
Costs incurred to generate third party income	–	–	–	67.4	67.4
Other content related spend	**87.4**	**–**	**22.3**	**391.9**	**501.6**
Restructuring costs	–	–	–	23.1	23.1
Total UK PSB Group content expenditure	**2,530.1**	**221.8**	**675.4**	**415.0**	**3,842.3**

Notes to the accounts (*Continued*)

Digital switchover (Digital UK Limited)	–	–	–	12.5	12.5
Digital switchover (DSHS Limited)	–	–	–	44.4	44.4
Total UK PSB Group expenditure	2,530.1	221.8	675.4	471.9	3,899.2
Lease reclassification****	–	–	–	(81.9)	(81.9)
UK PSB Group expenditure	2,530.1	221.8	675.4	390.0	3,817.3

* Included within BBC News channel are production costs of £26.8million, Newsgathering costs of £21.2million and other costs of £0.7million (2013: production costs of £27.2million, Newsgathering costs of £17.8million and other costs of £0.2million).

** BBC Online spend is monitored by annexe (relating to editorial areas of the service). Non-annexe spend covers costs relating to central editorial activities such as the BBC Homepage, technologies which operate across the service and overheads. The spend for each annexe was: News, Sport & Weather £47.8million (2013: £43.8million), Childrens £9.3million (2013: £8.5million), Knowledge & Learning £15.7million (2013: £18.7million), TV & iPlayer £11.1million (2013: £12.2million) and Audio & Music £11.7million (2013: £13.3million), giving a total annexe spend of £95.6million (2013: £96.5million). Non-annexe spend was £10.9million (2013: £6.5million).

*** Under the terms of the latest licence fee agreement, the BBC has committed to contribute funding toward broadband rollout across the UK and funding for the development of Local TV channels.

****In order to reflect the full cost of the UK PSB Group expenditure by service, finance lease interest is included, although it is not included in the Group operating expenditure.

B3.2 UK PSB Group infrastructure/support costs

Infrastructure/support costs include the following:

	2014 £m	2013 £m
Property	141.2	181.6
HR and training	38.6	45.4
Policy and strategy	9.1	12.0
Finance and operations	70.3	67.7
Marketing, audiences and communication	71.9	68.7
Total central costs	331.1	375.4
Technology*	130.3	175.1
Libraries, learning support and community events	32.0	33.6
Divisional running costs	62.7	64.5
BBC Trust Unit	12.0	11.9
Other	20.7	14.9
Total infrastructure/support costs	588.8	675.4

* Comparatives include the £51.7million impairment of DMI. See Note B1 for further details.

B4 Analysis of total operating costs by non-UK PSB entities

B4.1 Commercial activities

	Note	BBC Worldwide 2014 £m	BBC Worldwide 2013 £m	Other Commercials 2014 £m	Other Commercials 2013 £m	Total Commercials 2014 £m	Total Commercials 2013 £m
Cost of sales		524.7	557.7	118.9	121.6	643.6	679.3
Distribution costs		86.1	126.7	–	–	86.1	126.7
Administrative expenses		167.3	178.3	11.2	20.0	178.5	198.3
Total operating costs	A1	778.1	862.7	130.1	141.6	908.2	1,004.3

B4.2 BBC World Service and BBC Monitoring

	Note	2014 £m	2013 £m
Cost of sales		1.4	1.4
Distribution costs		27.3	33.8
Administrative expenses		243.5	272.4
Total operating costs	A1	272.2	307.6

ITV FINANCIAL STATEMENTS

Consolidated Income Statement

For the year ended 31 December	Note	2013 £m	2012 (restated) £m
Revenue	2.1	**2,389**	2,196
Operating costs		**(1,843)**	(1,750)
Operating profit		**546**	446
Presented as:			
Earnings before interest, tax, amortisation (EBITA) before exceptional items	2.1	**620**	513
Operating exceptional items	2.2	**(8)**	(7)
Amortisation and impairment of intangible assets	3.3	**(66)**	(60)
Operating profit		**546**	446
Financing income	4.4	**10**	20
Financing costs	4.4	**(125)**	(126)
Net financing costs	4.4	**(115)**	(106)
Share of losses of joint ventures and associated undertakings	2.1	**(2)**	(1)
Loss on sale and impairment of non-current assets (exceptional items)	2.2	**–**	(6)
Gain on sale and impairment of subsidiaries and investments (exceptional items)	2.2	**6**	1
Profit before tax		**435**	334
Taxation	2.3	**(105)**	(77)
Profit for the year		**330**	257
Profit attributable to:			
Owners of the Company		**326**	256
Non-controlling interests		**4**	1
Profit for the year		**330**	257
Earnings per share			
Basic earnings per share	2.4	**8.3p**	6.6p
Diluted earnings per share	2.4	**8.1p**	6.4p

Consolidated Statement of Financial Position

As at 31 December	Note	2013 £m	2012 (restated) £m
Non-current assets			
Property, plant and equipment	3.2	259	156
Intangible assets	3.3	954	938
Investments in joint ventures and associated undertakings		4	6
Available for sale financial assets		–	3
Held to maturity investments	4.1	–	145
Derivative financial instruments	4.3	41	99
Distribution rights	3.1.1	10	17
Net deferred tax asset	2.3	52	93
		1,320	1,457
Current assets			
Programme rights and other inventory	3.1.2	322	252
Trade and other receivables due within one year	3.1.4	388	366
Trade and other receivables due after more than one year	3.1.4	14	14
Trade and other receivables		402	380
Derivative financial instruments	4.3	32	–
Cash and cash equivalents	4.1	518	690
		1,274	1,322
Assets held for sale	3.5	–	25
		1,274	1,347
Current liabilities			
Borrowings	4.2	(62)	(7)
Derivative financial instruments	4.3	(6)	(1)
Trade and other payables due within one year	3.1.5	(702)	(622)
Trade payables due after more than one year	3.1.6	(42)	(31)
Trade and other payables		(744)	(653)
Current tax liabilities		(36)	(29)
Provisions	3.6	(19)	(25)
		(867)	(715)
Net current assets		407	632
Non-current liabilities			
Borrowings	4.2	(318)	(632)
Derivative financial instruments	4.3	(27)	(48)
Defined benefit pension deficit	3.7	(445)	(551)
Other payables		(40)	(14)
Provisions	3.6	(8)	(12)
		(838)	(1,257)
Net assets		889	832
Attributable to equity shareholders of the parent company			
Share capital	4.7.1	403	391
Share premium	4.7.1	174	122
Merger and other reserves	4.7.2	248	283
Translation reserve		7	13
Available for sale reserve		4	7
Retained earnings		22	1
Total equity attributable to equity shareholders of the parent company		858	817
Non-controlling interests		31	15
Total equity		889	832

Ian Griffiths
Group Finance Director

Notes to the accounts

Trade and other receivables can be analysed as follows:

	2013 £m	2012 (restated) £m
Due within one year:		
Trade receivables	295	264
Other receivables	40	44
Prepayments and accrued income	53	58
	388	366
Due after more than one year:		
Trade receivables	11	14
Other receivables	3	–
Total trade and other receivables	402	380

£306 million (2012: £278 million) of total trade receivables that are not impaired are aged as follows:

	2013 £m	2012 £m
Current	296	274
Up to 30 days overdue	8	2
Between 30 and 90 days overdue	2	2
	306	278

The balance above is stated net of a provision of £7 million (2012: £7 million) for impairment of trade receivables. Of the provision total, £3 million relates to balances overdue by more than 90 days (2012: £4 million) and £4 million relates to current balances (2012: £3 million).

Movements in the Group's provision for impairment of trade receivables can be shown as follows:

	2013 £m	2012 £m
At 1 January	7	11
Charged during the year	1	3
Receivables written off during the year as uncollectable (utilisation of provision)	(1)	(4)
Unused amounts reversed	–	(3)
At 31 December	7	7

3.1.5 Trade and other payables due within one year
Accounting policies
Trade payables are recognised at the value of the invoice received from a supplier.

The carrying value of trade payables is considered to approximate fair value.

Trade and other payables due within one year can be analysed as follows:

	2013 £m	2012 (restated) £m
Trade payables	43	34
Social security	7	7
Other payables	216	193
Accruals and deferred income	436	388
	702	622

3.1.6 Trade payables due after more than one year
Trade payables due after more than one year can be analysed as follows:

	2013 £m	2012 (restated) £m
Trade payables	42	31

This primarily relates to film creditors for which payment is due after more than one year.

3.1.7 Working capital management
Cash and working capital management continues to be a key focus. During the year the cash outflow from working capital was £15 million (2012: inflow of £1 million) derived as follows:

	2013 £m	2012 £m
(Increase)/decrease in programme rights and other inventory and distribution rights	(42)	29
(Increase)/decrease in receivables	(15)	17
Increase/(decrease) in payables	42	(45)
Working capital (outflow)/ inflow	(15)	1

The working capital outflow for the year excludes the impact of balances acquired on the purchase of new subsidiaries (see note 3.4).

The increase in programme rights and other inventory is largely driven by an increase in commissions and sports rights. The broadcast sports rights mainly represent payment for the FIFA World Cup and Rugby World Cup.

The increase in receivables has been driven by higher revenues, compared to December 2012, resulting in an increase in trade receivables.

The increase in payables primarily relates to trade payables, and an increase in the Group VAT liability.

SKY FINANCIAL STATEMENTS

Consolidated financial statements

Consolidated income statement
for the year ended 30 June 2014

	Notes	2014 £m	2013 £m
Revenue	2	7,632	7,235
Operating expense	3	(6,471)	(5,944)
Operating profit		1,161	1,291
Share of results of joint ventures and associates	13	35	46
Investment income	4	26	28
Finance costs	4	(140)	(108)
Profit before tax	5	1,082	1,257
Taxation	7	(217)	(278)
Profit for the year attributable to equity shareholders of the parent company		865	979
Earnings per share from profit for the year (in pence)			
Basic	8	55.4p	60.7p
Diluted	8	54.9p	59.7p

The accompanying notes are an integral part of this consolidated income statement.

All results relate to continuing operations.

Consolidated statement of comprehensive income
for the year ended 30 June 2014

	2014 £m	2013 £m
Profit for the year attributable to equity shareholders of the parent company	865	979
Other comprehensive income		
Amounts recognised directly in equity that may subsequently be recycled to the income statement		
Gain on revaluation of available-for-sale investments	104	186
Loss on cash flow hedges	(176)	(27)
Tax on cash flow hedges	39	7
	(33)	166
Amounts reclassified and reported in the income statement		
Gain (loss) on cash flow hedges	137	(48)
Tax on cash flow hedges	(31)	11
	106	(37)
Other comprehensive income for the year (net of tax)	73	129
Total comprehensive income for the year attributable to equity shareholders of the parent company	938	1,108

All results relate to continuing operations.

Consolidated Financial Statements

Consolidated balance sheet
as at 30 June 2014

	Notes	2014 £m	2013 £m
Non-current assets			
Goodwill	10	1,019	999
Intangible assets	11	810	718
Property, plant and equipment	12	1,088	1,041
Investments in joint ventures and associates	13	173	164
Available-for-sale investments	14	533	422
Deferred tax assets	15	31	38
Programme distribution rights	16	20	17
Trade and other receivables	17	7	17
Derivative financial assets	21	195	360
		3,876	3,776
Current assets			
Inventories	16	546	548
Trade and other receivables	17	635	591
Short-term deposits	21	295	595
Cash and cash equivalents	21	1,082	815
Derivative financial assets	21	15	20
		2,573	2,569
Total assets		**6,449**	**6,345**
Current liabilities			
Borrowings	20	11	11
Trade and other payables	18	2,286	2,023
Current tax liabilities		128	176
Provisions	19	48	94
Derivative financial liabilities	21	46	13
		2,519	2,317
Non-current liabilities			
Borrowings	20	2,658	2,909
Trade and other payables	18	56	63
Provisions	19	14	14
Derivative financial liabilities	21	129	29
Deferred tax liabilities	15	1	1
		2,858	3,016
Total liabilities		**5,377**	**5,333**
Share capital	23	781	797
Share premium	24	1,437	1,437
Reserves	24	(1,146)	(1,222)
Total equity attributable to equity shareholders of the parent company	24	**1,072**	**1,012**
Total liabilities and shareholders' equity		**6,449**	**6,345**

The accompanying notes are an integral part of this consolidated balance sheet.

These consolidated financial statements of British Sky Broadcasting Group plc, registered number 02247735, have been approved and authorised for issue by the Board of Directors on 25 July 2014 and were signed on its behalf by:

Jeremy Darroch　　　　**Andrew Griffith**
Chief Executive Officer　　Chief Financial Officer

Notes to the accounts

17. Trade and other receivables

	2014 £m	2013 £m
Gross trade receivables	235	163
Less: provision for impairment of receivables	(95)	(89)
Net trade receivables	**140**	**74**
Amounts receivable from joint ventures and associates	7	8
Amounts receivable from other related parties	5	7
Prepayments	279	309
Accrued income	179	162
VAT	2	1
Other	23	30
Current trade and other receivables	**635**	**591**
Prepayments	4	6
Other receivables	3	11
Non-current trade and other receivables	**7**	**17**
Total trade and other receivables	**642**	**608**

Included within current trade and other receivables is nil (2013: nil) which is due in more than one year.

The ageing of the Group's net trade receivables which are past due but not impaired is as follows:

	2014 £m	2013 £m
Up to 30 days past due date	107	52
30 to 60 days past due date	4	5
60 to 120 days past due date	2	2
	113	59

The Directors consider that the carrying amount of trade and other receivables approximates their fair values. The Group is exposed to credit risk on its trade and other receivables, however the Group does not have any significant concentrations of credit risk, with exposure spread over a large number of counterparties and customers. Trade receivables principally comprise amounts outstanding from subscribers, advertisers and other customers.

Provisions for doubtful debts

	2014 £m	2013 £m
Balance at beginning of year	89	89
Amounts utilised	(27)	(36)
Provided during the year	33	36
Balance at end of year	**95**	**89**

Notes to the accounts

18. Trade and other payables

	2014 £m	2013 £m
Trade payables[i]	802	712
Amounts owed to joint ventures and associates	11	9
Amounts owed to other related parties	124	102
VAT	169	143
Accruals	747	685
Deferred income	318	295
Other	115	77
Current trade and other payables	**2,286**	**2,023**
Trade payables	23	18
Amounts owed to other related parties	10	–
Deferred income	5	9
Other	18	36
Non-current trade and other payables	**56**	**63**
Total trade and other payables	**2,342**	**2,086**

(i)   Included within trade payables are £213 million (2013: £225 million) of US dollar-denominated payables.

The Directors consider that the carrying amount of trade and other payables approximates their fair values. Trade payables principally comprise amounts outstanding for programming purchases and ongoing costs.

19. Provisions

	At 1 July 2012 £m	Reclassified during the year £m	Provided (released) during the year £m	Utilised during the year £m	At 1 July 2013 £m	Provided during the year £m	Utilised during the year £m	At 30 June 2014
Current liabilities								
Restructuring provision[i]	6	–	13	(3)	16	14	(8)	22
Acquired and acquisition-related provisions[ii]	15	(1)	(14)	–	–	–	–	–
Customer-related provisions[iii]	–	–	47	(6)	41	–	(39)	2
Other provisions[iv]	22	17	17	(19)	37	6	(19)	24
	43	16	63	(28)	94	20	(66)	48
Non-current liabilities								
Other provisions[v]	12	2	6	(6)	14	10	(10)	14

(i)   These provisions significantly relate to costs incurred as part of corporate efficiency programmes.
(ii) These provisions arose on the acquisition of Amstrad which took place during the year ended 30 June 2008.
(iii) These provisions are for those costs incurred in the one-off upgrade of set-top boxes and the programme to offer wireless connectors to selected Sky Movies customers.
(iv) Included in other provisions are amounts provided for legal disputes and warranty liabilities.
(v)   Included within non-current other provisions are amounts provided for onerous contracts for property leases and maintenance. The timing of the cash flows are dependent on the terms of the leases, but are expected to continue up to August 2016.

Notes to the accounts (*Continued*)

2. Revenue

	2014 £m	2013 £m
Retail subscription	6,255	5,951
Wholesale subscription	422	396
Advertising	472	440
Installation, hardware and service	85	87
Other	398	361
	7,632	7,235

Revenue arises from goods and services provided to the UK, with the exception of £478 million (2013: £461 million) which arises from services provided to other countries. Included within wholesale subscription revenue for the year ended 30 June 2014 is £15 million credit received following the termination of an escrow agreement with a current wholesale operator.

3. Operating expense

	2014 £m	2013 £m
Programming	2,662	2,487
Direct networks	850	686
Marketing	1,215	1,117
Subscriber management and supply chain	694	673
Transmission, technology and fixed networks	460	405
Administration	590	576
	6,471	5,944

Included within operating expenses for the year ended 30 June 2014 are:
- Costs of £72 million relating to the acquisition and integration of the O2 consumer broadband and fixed-line telephony business, including amortisation of £27 million in relation to associated intangible assets. The costs have been recognised as follows:
  - £31 million within direct networks
  - £24 million within administration
  - £13 million within transmission, technology and fixed networks
  - £3 million within subscriber management and supply chain
  - £1 million within marketing.
- Costs of £40 million relating to a corporate restructuring and efficiency programme in the current year including an impairment of £2 million in relation to associated intangible and tangible assets. These costs have been recognised as follows:
  - £22 million within administration
  - £15 million within marketing
  - £3 million within subscriber management and supply chain.
- Costs of £2 million as a result of the termination of an escrow agreement with a current wholesale operator. This cost has been recognised within administration.

Included within operating expenses for the year ended 30 June 2013 are:
- Credit of £32 million relating to a credit note received following an Ofcom determination. This credit has been recognised within direct networks.
- Credit of £33 million relating to the final settlement of disputes with a former manufacturer of set-top boxes, net of associated costs and including an impairment of £6 million in relation to associated intangible assets. This credit has been recognised within subscriber management and supply chain.
- Costs of £31 million relating to the one-off upgrade of set-top boxes. The costs have been recognised within subscriber management and supply chain.
- Costs of £25 million relating to a programme to offer wireless connectors to selected Sky Movies customers. The costs have been recognised within subscriber management and supply chain.
- Costs of £15 million relating to the acquisition and integration of the O2 consumer broadband and fixed-line telephony business, including amortisation of £4 million in relation to associated intangible assets. The costs have been recognised as follows:
  - £7 million within administration
  - £3 million within direct networks
  - £3 million within transmission, technology and fixed networks
  - £2 million within subscriber management and supply chain.
- Costs of £33 million relating to a corporate efficiency programme in the prior year including an impairment of £6 million in relation to associated intangible and tangible assets. The costs have been recognised as follows:
  - £29 million within administration
  - £1 million within programming
  - £1 million within marketing
  - £1 million within subscriber management and supply chain
  - £1 million within transmission, technology and fixed networks.

Here are the ratios for the three companies accounts calculated according to the formulae listed on page 83–84.

The first thing to note is that whenever you review financial statements, the figures are as at the year-end date. Things may have changed in the intervening period, so it's important to bear in mind any knowledge you have of events that have occurred since that are significant enough to affect company results. All the calculations and commentary that follow are based on the information available in the published accounts only.

The Cost of Sales isn't quoted directly on the face of the Income Statement for any of the companies. For the BBC, information has been estimated from a number of notes reproduced (notes B3.1, B4.1 and B4.2). For Sky, the cost of sales estimate has come from just the programming costs and direct network costs (from note 3 reproduced on the previous page). For ITV, no notes detailed the Cost of Sales, so some of the ratios are impossible to calculate.

Debtors and creditors included on the face of the Statement of Financial Position are often quoted as 'Trade *and other* receivables' and 'Trade *and other* payables'. This indicates that you shouldn't use these figures directly from the Statement of Financial Position, instead check the note and use just the trade receivables and trade payables (ignoring all 'others'). These notes are also reproduced for you on the previous pages.

COACH'S TIP

The point of the debtor days' and creditor days' ratios are to establish how long it takes to receive trade income and to pay trade suppliers, so it's important not to let 'other' payables or receivables distort the ratios.

You may wish to practise calculating a few of these ratios for yourself to check that you can find the correct numbers to use from the accounts on the previous pages.

Ratio	BBC For the year ended 31/3/		ITV For the year ended 31/12/		Sky For the year ended 30/6/	
	2014	2013	2013	2012	2014	2013
Gross Margin*	41.5%	38.8%			53.9%	56.1%
Expenses*	35.1%	34.8%			38.8%	34.2%
Operating Profit Margin	6.5%	3.9%	22.9%	20.3%	15.2%	17.8%
Net Profit Margin	3.0%	3.1%	13.8%	11.7%	11.3%	13.5%
Return on Capital Employed (ROCE)	24.9%	18.4%	45.2%	30.5%	31.1%	32.9%
Stock Days*	90.1	75.4			56.7	63.0
Debtor Days	15.7	16.0	45.1	43.9	6.7	3.7
Creditor Days*	52.4	51.9			83.4	81.9
Current Ratio	2.2	1.9	1.5	1.8	1.0	1.1
Quick Ratio	1.5	1.3	1.1	1.5	0.8	0.9
Gearing	76.6%	96.3%	26.3%	43.2%	71.3%	74.2%
Interest Cover (operating profit / interest)	2.0	1.4	4.4	3.5	8.3	11.9

* the cost of sales has been estimated where possible from various notes to the accounts – no total cost of sales vs expenses split is published by any of these companies. Being an estimate, these ratios are not to be fully relied upon, instead they are only a guide.

🗩🗩 COACHING SESSION 10

What reasons can you think of for the differences in each company's results? And how does this fit with the SC&I parts of our original analysis? Make a note of your thoughts beneath each ratio.

Ratio	BBC For the year ended 31/3/		ITV For the year ended 31/12/		Sky For the year ended 30/6	
	2014	2013	2013	2012	2014	2013
Gross Margin	41.5%	38.8%			53.9%	56.1%
Expenses	35.1%	34.8%			38.8%	34.2%
Operating Profit Margin	6.5%	3.9%	22.9%	20.3%	15.2%	17.8%
Net Profit Margin	3.0%	3.1%	13.8%	11.7%	11.3%	13.5%
Return on Capital Employed (ROCE)	24.9%	18.4%	45.2%	30.4%	31.1%	32.9%
Stock Days	90.1	75.4			56.7	63.0

Debtor Days	15.7	16.0	45.1	43.9	6.7	3.7
Creditor Days	52.4	51.9			83.4	81.9
Current Ratio	2.2	1.9	1.5	1.8	1.0	1.1
Quick Ratio	1.5	1.3	1.1	1.5	0.8	0.9
Gearing	76.6%	96.3%	26.3%	43.2%	71.3%	74.2%
Interest Cover (EBIT / interest)	2.0	1.4	4.4	3.5	8.3	11.9

SUGGESTED SOLUTION TO COACHING SESSION 10

Ratio	
Gross Margin	Gross margin will be lower for the BBC because it is a not-for-profit organisation with a restricted amount of funding coming from the licence fee.
Expenses	Whilst all companies will have a cost control focus, the BBC may have lower expenses because they are publicly funded and restricted by the licence fee income and because they have no requirement to invest for growth, whereas Sky may spend more to achieve growth.
Operating Profit Margin	As discussed above, the BBC will have lower margins. ITV are working on improving their results and have the highest margin here. Sky may be spending more to grow their business. For example some of their investment in new products, services and markets may not be able to be capitalised. If so, this would increase their annual costs. In addition Sky's communications business will have lower margins.
Net Profit Margin	The two commercial providers are very similar here, once again the BBC has such a different funding model. However the BBC will still make surpluses to re-invest in future programming or new technologies.
Return on Capital Employed (ROCE)	The BBC has very low capital employed because there are no shareholders, so no share capital within their equity, only retained surpluses; hence the high ROCE shown here. ITV are clearly managing the business to provide high returns. Sky may show lower returns because of the lower operating margin (see notes above).
Stock Days	Stock days represent the partially produced programmes and programmes not yet matched against revenues. The figures are similar for each company.
Debtor Days	The publicly funded BBC will have low debtor days as customers pay their licence fees as required or by direct debit. Sky also have a direct debit subscription service, so again debtors are low. ITV rely much more on advertising revenues, hence the higher debtor days as advertisers take longer credit terms.

Creditor Days	Creditor days are usually best judged against an industry average, but with only two companies' results to compare, it is hard to comment on the reasons for the differences. Remember, these ratios are affected by the estimated cost of sales figure, so without more accurate information, it's difficult to comment on the differences.
Current Ratio	All companies shown are relatively cash rich and highly liquid leaving us with no concerns about their day to day viability.
Quick Ratio	As above
Gearing	Gearing is high for the BBC purely because there is very little equity (as mentioned above equity is purely retained surpluses), so this is not a concern. Gearing for ITV was relatively high in 2012, but they have resolved the situation in 2013. Gearing for Sky is also high but the interest cover is very strong (see below), so not a concern.
Interest Cover	Despite the BBC keeping surpluses to a minimum, they are more than able to pay the interest costs. Even if surpluses halve, there is enough operating profit to cover it. Sky have a very strong interest cover, as mentioned above.

You may wish to conduct this analysis on:

- Customers; to make sure they can pay.

- Suppliers; to make sure they will be around in the future to supply you.

- Competitors; to establish the state of the market and whether it is an attractive proposition for you to enter the market, to benchmark against their costs as a double check for your budgeting and to establish how you can manage your business in a different way or in a more cost effective way.

COACHING SESSION 11

Start your SCIRE analysis now with the SCI sections:

Section	Questions to ask / information to find	Analysis of the situation
Sector To start with, simply brainstorm everything that you know about the industry, ask people who might have some knowledge of the industry and do some internet research	Is it growing or is it in decline?	
	Is it very competitive with many commodity providers, or is it very differentiated?	
	Is there much consolidation in the industry (companies acquiring each other)?	
	What is the business model (where are most of the costs in the industry – in cost of sales or in overheads)?	
	Have there been any one-off events affecting the industry?	
	Is the business growing or in decline?	
Company To start with, simply brainstorm everything that you know about the company, ask people who might have some knowledge and do some internet research	Is the business a high end provider with a differentiated product or mainly competing on cost leadership?	
	Are they an innovative company launching new products?	
	What kind of assets does this company hold?	
Information Available Chairman's / directors' reports, website	Review the company strategy and market commentary; does it line up with what you thought in the previous two sections?	

⌓⌓ COACHING SESSION 12

You may wish to calculate the ratios for a company you're interested in now (it's good to compare two years in order to see if things are improving or not).

If you can find any additional information that would help you to get an idea of specific costs, calculate each cost type as a percentage of sales – for example, advertising, royalties, product development, etc.

If you prefer, there are companies that provide this information for you:

http://www.dnb.co.uk/scores-data

http://www.experian.co.uk/business-express/protecting-you-from-financial-risk/protect-overview.html?gclid=CMSN9PrvhsMCFUXKtAodt0wAJw

Two options are given above, but there are many others; you can perform an internet search for 'credit reference agency'.

Ratio	Calculation	Current Year	Comparison Previous Year
Profitability on Sales			
Gross Margin	$\dfrac{\text{Gross Profit}}{\text{Sales Revenue}} \times 100$		
Expenses	$\dfrac{\text{Expenses}}{\text{Sales Revenue}} \times 100$		
Operating Profit Margin	$\dfrac{\text{Operating Profit (EBIT)}}{\text{Sales Revenue}} \times 100$		
Net Profit Margin	$\dfrac{\text{Net Profit}}{\text{Sales Revenue}} \times 100$		
Return on Investment			
Return on Capital Employed (ROCE)	$\dfrac{\text{Net Profit}}{\text{(Total Equity + Non-Current Borrowings)}} \times 100$		

Measures of Efficiency			
Stock Days	$\dfrac{\text{Inventory}}{\text{Cost of Sales}} \times 365$		
Debtor Days	$\dfrac{\text{Accounts Receivable}}{\text{Sales Revenue}} \times 365$		
Creditor Days	$\dfrac{\text{Accounts Payable}}{\text{Cost of Sales}} \times 365$		
Liquidity Ratios			
Current Ratio	$\dfrac{\text{Current Assets}}{\text{Current Liabilities}}$		
Quick Ratio	$\dfrac{\text{Current Assets}}{\text{Inventory Current Liabilities}}$		
Risk			
Gearing	$\dfrac{\text{Non-Current Borrowings}}{(\text{Total Equity} + \text{Non-Current Borrowings})} \times 100$		
Any Additional Ratios:			

Don't forget to complete the final stage of SCIRE analysis with the overall evaluation. What have you learned?

Section	Questions to ask / information to find	Analysis of the situation
Evaluation Put together all the information gathered in the previous sections	What did you determine about the industry and the company?	
	What did you discover about the company from the written statements supporting the published accounts and from your internet search?	
	Did the ratios line up with what you expected to see?	
	Did the written statements and the figures and ratios tell the same story?	
	What is your overall evaluation of the business?	

ONLINE RESOURCE

A downloadable SCIRE analysis template and ratio calculator is available at:

www.TYCoachbooks.com/Finance

NEXT STEPS

In this section you have:

• Evaluated businesses in different industries, established what you expect to see in their accounts, and compared their view and actual performance to your expectations.

In the next section we will look at how groups work and what we need to understand about them if we wish to trade with a subsidiary of a group.

 **TAKEAWAYS**

This is your opportunity to take stock of what you've learned from this chapter. You might now want to choose other chapters and exercises to focus on, or you can continue to work through the whole book if this better fits your needs.

1. Which companies did you review to compare ratios?

_____

_____

_____

_____

_____

_____

_____

_____

2. How did the companies compare?

_____

_____

_____

_____

_____

_____

_____

_____

3. What reasons can you think of for differences in performance, efficiency or health?

_____

_____

_____

_____

_____

_____

_____

_____

_____

_____

4. What can you learn about how to improve your company results from this?

_____

_____

_____

_____

_____

_____

_____

_____

_____

_____

6 HOW DO GROUPS WORK?

 OUTCOMES FROM THIS CHAPTER

- In this chapter we will look at:
    - How groups are structured
    - How group accounts are consolidated
    - What we need to understand if we are looking to trade with a subsidiary of a group

Self-test quiz:

1. What is a group?

    ▪

2. What is the difference between a parent and a holding company?

    ▪

3. What is a subsidiary?

    ▪

4. What is an associate?

    ▪

5. What is an investment?

    ▪

6. What is a non-controlling interest?

    ▪

7. What is a transfer price?

    ▪

Suggested solutions:

1. What is a group?

   ■ A group is a collection of parent and subsidiary entities that are controlled as a single economic entity

2. What is the difference between a parent and a holding company?

   ■ A holding company does not trade in its own right, only functioning to buy and sell other entities. A parent company trades in its own right

3. What is a subsidiary?

   ■ A subsidiary is controlled by a parent or holding company, owning more than 50% of the shares

4. What is an associate?

   ■ A parent company has significant influence over an associated company, owning between 20% and 50% of the shares

5. What is an investment?

   ■ An investment is a small holding of shares in another company of less than 20%

6. What is a non-controlling interest?

   ■ It is the proportion of a business owned by a company other than the controlling parent company

7. What is a transfer price?

   ■ The transfer price is the price charged when trading occurs between companies within a group

Here's an example group of companies:

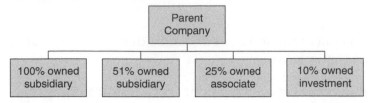

- Any company that is more than 50% owned by a parent is known as a subsidiary. The parent has overall control.

- If a parent owns between 20% and 50% of a company, then that company is known as an associate. The parent has significant influence, but not overall control.

- A company with a parent owning less than 20% is just a fixed asset investment.

A group will publish accounts, including line-by-line, 100% of all the results of the parent company plus subsidiaries, whether the subsidiary is wholly owned or not. Where 100% of a company's results are included, but part of that company is owned outside the group, then a one line disclosure is made labelled '**profit or loss attributable to non-controlling interest**'.

Any associate companies' results will be included as a single line labelled '**due from associates**' just before the operating profit (EBIT) line in the Income Statement.

Small holdings (less than 20%) will show as a fixed asset investment in the Statement of Financial Position and as dividends received in the Income Statement.

The difficulty arises in analysing subsidiary accounts when different subsidiaries trade with each other.

Imagine this situation where Company A sells products to Company B.

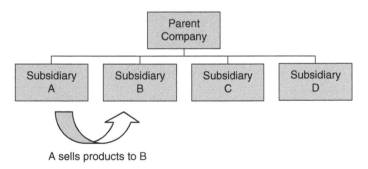

A sells products to B

At what price should A sell to B? The 'transfer price' should be the market price, treating the sale as if it were to any other non-group company. However, let's imagine that Company A is in a country with a very high tax rate and Company B is in a country with a low tax rate, the temptation would be to sell at a very low price, so that A makes almost no profit and therefore reduces its tax burden, but B makes more profit but only pays a low rate of tax.

Different companies treat this intercompany trading differently:

- Some will actively minimise their tax bill.

- Some will make 'arms-length' arrangements: selling at market prices, but internally making decisions on where to produce goods for different markets to keep tax bills to an optimum level.

- Some will trade truly at arms-length.

In addition to this, companies have been known to use other methods to minimise tax bills by:

- Charging head office overheads to the subsidiaries using a basis that means a higher charge to those in high tax countries.

- Charging a licence fee to subsidiaries to use logos, marketing information, etc. to raise costs in high tax countries.

- Structuring companies to have head offices overseas so that all operations are controlled away from high tax countries.

Our problem arises when trading with a subsidiary. It is impossible to tell what approach the group takes.

If you wish to trade with A, they may look as though they make very little profit and you may be concerned about their viability.

If you wish to trade with B, they look very profitable indeed. However, if later the group sells B, their trading arrangements may change and you find that B is not such a safe bet!

A group or parent company has no liability to support a subsidiary in trouble, and no compulsion to settle the debts of a subsidiary that goes into liquidation (unless it has given parent company guarantees to its trading partners).

 COACH'S TIP

The best approaches to take when wishing to trade with a subsidiary of a group of companies are:

- Evaluate the accounts of the subsidiary with which you wish to trade.

- Evaluate the accounts of the group.

- Try to gain a parent company guarantee if you have any doubts about the subsidiary.

- Try to establish whether the subsidiary is strategically important to the group; if it supplies a scarce resource to the group, if it provides an important service in the supply chain, if it brings any competitive advantage to the group, then perhaps you can be more confident that it will remain a part of the group.

→ NEXT STEPS

In this section you have:

- Understood how subsidiary company's accounts are included in groups.

- Understood the difficulties in knowing the real performance of a subsidiary.

- Considered approaches to trading with subsidiaries.

In the next section we will look at what to expect from an audit.

TAKEAWAYS

This is your opportunity to take stock of what you've learned from this chapter. You might now want to choose other chapters and exercises to focus on, or you can continue to work through the whole book if this better fits your needs.

1. What subsidiaries of groups do you work with?

_____

_____

_____

_____

_____

_____

_____

_____

_____

2. What can you learn by looking at both their accounts and the group accounts?

_____

_____

_____

_____

_____

_____

_____

_____

_____

_____

3. What level of risk are you exposed to in trading with these subsidiaries?

_____

_____

_____

_____

_____

_____

_____

_____

4. What actions can you take to protect your business?

_____

_____

_____

_____

_____

_____

_____

_____

_____

7 | I'VE GOT AN AUDIT COMING UP

 OUTCOMES FROM THIS CHAPTER

- In this chapter we will look at:
  - The need for an audit and the audit process
  - How auditors plan and carry out their work
  - What they're looking for and the information they will require
  - How to make sure that your processes are robust enough

WHAT IS AN AUDIT?

According to the Institute of Chartered Accountants in England and Wales (ICAEW), an audit has the following purpose:

> 'In law, the auditors are appointed by the shareholders of the company to provide them with an independent report. The report is required to state whether in the auditors' opinion the annual accounts (which are prepared by and are the responsibility of the board of directors) give a true and fair view in accordance with the relevant financial reporting framework.'
>
> (ICAEW, 2006).

For companies over a certain size, the audit is a legal requirement from the Companies Act 2006. To be exempt from audit, a company must meet two out of the following three criteria for two consecutive years:

- Annual turnover must be £6.5 million or less.

- The balance sheet total must be £3.26 million or less.

- The average number of employees must be 50 or fewer.

Certain types of companies, such as banks, cannot be exempt from audit even if they meet the criteria. Companies that are exempt from being audited can still choose to have their financial statements audited. Many will do so as there are many benefits to having an audit, which we will look at later in this chapter.

Definitions

An audit can be defined as:

'The purpose of the statutory audit is to provide an independent opinion to the shareholders on the truth and fairness of the financial statements, whether they have been properly prepared in accordance with the Companies Act and to report by exception to the shareholders on the other requirements of company law such as where, in the auditors' opinion, proper accounting records have not been kept.'

ICAEW, 2006, 'AuditQualityQa
Fundamentals – Audit purpose'.

Key concepts for audit:

Investigation	The role of the auditor is to investigate a company's financial statements; the auditor performs audit tests to obtain evidence that the financial statements have been properly prepared. Auditors follow requirements from International Standards on Auditing (ISAs) when performing their work.
Reasonable assurance	The auditors will never be able to conclude that the financial statements are 100% accurate or that they are entirely free from error or misstatement. This is because the auditor cannot perform audit tests on every single transaction. Reasonable assurance gives some comfort but not a guarantee.
Truth and fairness	'True and fair' means that the financial statements are technically correct, conform to relevant regulations, are appropriately presented and are free from bias.
Independent	Independence and objectivity are the characteristics of the auditor, meaning that the audit opinion can be relied upon.
Report	The auditor has a legal obligation to issue an auditor's report, giving an opinion on the truth and fairness of the financial statements. The auditor's report must be presented with the company's financial statements to the shareholders and also placed on public record.

The key issue is that the auditor's report expresses an opinion on the financial statements. Assuming the opinion is favourable, shareholders and other people using the company's financial statements have confidence that the accounts have been properly prepared in accordance with all relevant regulations. This enhances the credibility of the accounts and makes them more trustworthy.

When an auditor cannot say that the financial statements are true and fair, usually because the accounts have not been properly prepared and contain a significant error, this is called an adverse opinion. This is very rare in practice, because almost always the management will amend the financial statements so that they are correct, thus avoiding the adverse opinion being issued. An adverse opinion creates a very bad impression of the company and of its management team. The shareholders would almost certainly act to remove the directors from office and bad publicity could affect the share price.

A common misconception is that the auditor is looking for frauds. This is not the case – it is the responsibility of management to prevent and detect frauds. The auditor may discover a fraud whilst carrying out audit procedures, but this is not the objective of the audit. If the auditor does uncover a fraud they will alert management (unless they think management is involved!) who will then take action against the fraudsters.

One of the key characteristics of the auditor is that they must be independent of the company they are auditing. There are many ethical rules that have to be followed by auditors, many of which are aimed at safeguarding the independence of the audit opinion. For example, an auditor cannot hold shares in a client company, have close personal relationships with employees at a client company, or enter into business arrangements with a client company. If any of these took place, the auditor would not be independent and this would undermine the credibility of the audit report and of the company's financial statements.

An audit can be very expensive and companies may be reluctant to pay. In 2014, the highest audit fee in the UK was £35 million – this was paid by Barclays to the audit firm PwC. The average audit fee is a lot lower, and small companies may only pay a few thousand pounds for their audit. Even when paying a small amount for the audit, companies will want to see some benefits. A few are listed below:

- During the audit, the auditor is likely to come across problems, and can make recommendations to improve business processes.

- The auditor can provide additional services to their clients such as tax planning.

- The auditor may spot frauds whilst carrying out audit procedures.

- Having an auditor's report can make it easier to raise finance and reduce the cost of borrowing.

WHAT IS THE PROCESS OF AN AUDIT?

The diagram shows the main stages in a typical audit, and each stage is explained below.

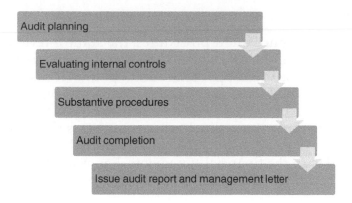

Audit planning

Planning includes performing a preliminary review of the financial statements to assess potential risks of error and developing and confirming an understanding of the business, especially new developments during the year under audit. ISAs require that audit planning is driven by risk assessment, and this is a crucial part of the audit. The point of risk assessment is to assess the areas of the financial statements that are at risk of error. Once these areas have been determined, the auditor can plan appropriate procedures in response.

Evaluating internal controls

Auditors are required to document, understand and evaluate the internal controls of their audit client. This process may reveal that controls are weak, indicating a higher risk of error in the financial statements. In this situation the auditor cannot place reliance on the client's systems and controls, and audit work needs to be very detailed. However, if the process reveals that the client has a good system of internal controls, the auditor can test the controls with the purpose of relying on them as a source of audit evidence. This is an efficient method of auditing.

Substantive procedures

The auditor must always perform substantive procedures (also known as tests of detail) on the balances and transactions recognised in the financial statements. These procedures are designed to provide evidence that the balances and transactions are complete, accurate, valid and disclosed properly. Substantive procedures provide the bulk of audit evidence in most audits, and can be time consuming to conduct. They are often performed on a sample basis.

Audit completion

After performing the planned audit procedures, the auditor reviews the results and conclusions of the procedures to ensure that sufficient appropriate evidence has been obtained to support the audit opinion. It may be that further procedures need to be conducted in some areas. At this stage, the auditor also reviews the final version of the financial statements and concludes on the going concern status of the client. An audit clearance meeting is held where any unresolved matters will be discussed. The auditor must also read any information that is to be issued with the financial statements. For example, the directors' report to ensure they are consistent.

Issue the audit report and management letter

The auditor's report is the key output of the audit. It must state whether, in the auditor's opinion, the financial statements show a true and fair view and have been properly prepared in accordance with the Companies Act. The auditor is also required to present a report to management (known as the **management letter**) in which any significant problems identified during the audit are explained, and recommendations for improvement are given. For example, the auditor may have found that better credit control is needed and will suggest improvements to that business process.

What information will the auditors be looking for?

The auditors have the right to ask for any information and explanations that are necessary – this right is given by the Companies Act. A person who makes a misleading, false or deceptive statement to the auditor can be prosecuted and face two years in prison! This applies to directors, managers and all employees of the audited company. It is therefore important to understand the sort of information that auditors will require and to give the correct information when asked.

Usually, when planning the audit, the auditor will discuss information requirements with the management team, who then try to make sure that the information is ready. This makes the audit process smoother and can save costs, as any delay in the audit field work means additional audit fees.

Every company is different, and therefore the information that the auditors will need will vary between audits. Remember that information is not always based on documents; auditors can obtain evidence through discussions and enquiries, so sometimes they will ask for a written confirmation of matters that have been talked through as part of the audit process. In general terms, for every audit the auditor would need the following information:

- An organisational structure showing key management personnel and responsibilities.

- A group structure detailing parent company and subsidiary relationships.

- Recent management accounts broken down into different business divisions or product lines.

- Information on major product lines, services offered, key competitors.

- Details of major contracts with customers and suppliers.

- Information on financing arrangements such as new borrowings taken out during the year and overdraft facilities.

- Systems documentation such as flow charts, diagrams or narrative descriptions.

- Reports issued by business functions such as the internal audit department and risk management team.

- Minutes of all board meetings held during the year.

- Details of any major legal situations such as court cases that the company is involved with.

- Information on related parties and any transactions with them (a related party is a person with a connection to the company, such as the spouse of a director).

- Details of any significant changes planned for the business such as major acquisitions or disposals, new product lines being developed and planned overseas expansion.

- Cash flow and profit forecasts and any other prospective financial information.

- Information on regulations with which the company is required to comply, for example health and safety rules.

This information will generally be required at the planning stage of the audit when the auditor is developing business understanding and assessing risk of error in the financial statements.

When the auditor is performing evaluation of controls and obtaining evidence by performing substantive procedures, more specific information will be needed for each area of the financial statements. Some examples are given below:

Area of the financial statements	Information required by the auditor
Non-current assets	<ul><li>Purchase invoices for capital expenditure</li><li>Evidence of approval of significant capital expenditure</li><li>Lease documentation for assets held under leasing arrangements</li><li>Insurance policies for major assets</li><li>The location of assets (the auditor will physically inspect a sample of assets)</li></ul>
Inventories	<ul><li>Stock-take instructions and locations</li><li>Stock movement reports</li><li>Details of any stock written off during the year</li><li>A sample of documentation such as delivery notes, goods received notes, purchase orders and invoices received</li><li>Details of any stock in transit at the year end</li><li>Details of any stock located away from the company's premises</li></ul>
Accounts receivable	<ul><li>Aged debtors listing</li><li>Details on credit control procedures</li><li>A sample of documentation such as customer orders and invoices raised</li><li>Details of significant debtors written off or with allowances against them</li><li>Correspondence with the customer where any significant balances are disputed</li></ul>
Bank and cash	<ul><li>All bank statements</li><li>Bank reconciliations performed during the year</li><li>Confirmation from the bank of all balances at the year end</li><li>Evidence of approval for significant cash payments</li><li>Any petty cash will be counted by the auditor</li></ul>
Borrowings	<ul><li>Loan agreements to confirm the loan amount and interest rate</li><li>Evidence of approval for loans taken out or paid off</li><li>Correspondence with the provider of finance (for example if the terms of an agreement have changed)</li></ul>
Accounts payable	<ul><li>Supplier statements</li><li>A sample of documentation such as purchase orders, invoices received, goods received notes</li><li>Correspondence with the supplier where any significant balances are disputed</li></ul>

COACH'S TIP

Find out as early as possible in the audit process the information that the auditor is likely to require from you. It is helpful to know if the auditor has pin-pointed any specific areas of risk, e.g. balances that are likely to contain errors, so that you are ready to provide the necessary explanations and evidence. Remember that the auditor is not looking to blame anyone if errors have occurred in the accounts – if the auditor finds a problem they will recommend improvements to make things run better in the future.

If you know that the auditor is going to discuss an issue with you, it is good to have all of the documentation ready. Some companies prepare files of information to assist the auditor in their work. For example, if you work in credit control, the auditor will probably want to discuss the level of debtors outstanding with you, so you could prepare a file containing a recent aged debtors' report and evidence showing what has been done to collect balances outstanding, such as correspondence with slow paying debtors.

Be aware that the auditor will ask to see original documentation rather than copies of documentation, as originals are a more reliable source of evidence for the auditor.

When obtaining evidence, the auditor may simply ask to observe a business process to see that it is functioning correctly. For example, the auditor will observe a stock count or the distribution of any wages paid in cash. The auditor may also ask to physically inspect assets, in which case you simply show them the asset so that they can record that it exists.

If your company has an internal audit department, the auditor may liaise with them when planning the audit as one of the roles of internal audit is to monitor the processes relating to financial accounting. In this case your internal audit team may gather together the necessary information for the auditor.

COACHING SESSION 13

What are the benefits of an audit to a company?	What are the downsides of an audit?

SUGGESTED SOLUTIONS TO COACHING SESSION 13

What are the benefits of an audit to a company?	What are the downsides of an audit?
• Enhances credibility of accounts	• The audit can be expensive
• Makes directors accountable for the accounts they produce	• Auditors can disrupt the business when staff are performing their work
• Auditors recommend improvements to the business	• There is little benefit of an audit for an owner-managed business with little external finance
• Audit procedures may uncover fraud	
• Auditors can offer other services such as tax planning	

NEXT STEPS

In this section you have:

• Understood the need for an audit and the audit process

• Seen how auditors plan and carry out their work

• Understood the type of information auditors will ask for

• Learned how to respond to requests for information from the auditor

In the next section we will move onto management accounting, looking at the information used internally within businesses to plan, control and make decisions.

TAKEAWAYS

This is your opportunity to take stock of what you've learned from this chapter. You might now want to choose other chapters and exercises to focus on, or you can continue to work through the whole book if this better fits your needs.

1. What information do you think your company's auditors would need in order to plan the audit?

_____

_____

_____

_____

_____

_____

_____

2. How can you plan to ensure that you respond to the auditors' requests for information quickly and accurately?

_____

_____

_____

_____

_____

_____

_____

_____

3. Do you think there are specific areas within your business that the auditors would be likely to consider as high risk, and can anything be done to improve them before the audit?

_____

_____

_____

_____

_____

_____

_____

_____

_____

PART 2
MANAGEMENT ACCOUNTING

8

HOW DOES THE FINANCE DEPARTMENT ACCOUNT FOR COSTS?

 OUTCOMES FROM THIS CHAPTER

- In this chapter we will review:
    - The classification of costs
    - How costs behave
    - Two different methods commonly used for costing for control and for decision making

Self-test quiz:

1. What different ways can you think of to categorise costs?

    -
    -
    -
    -

2. What is the definition of a variable cost?

    -

3. Give an example of a variable cost.

    -

4. Give an example of a fixed cost.

    -

5. Give an example of a semi-fixed/semi-variable cost.

    -

6. Draw a graph of a stepped cost.

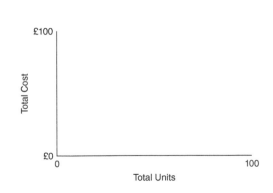

Suggested solutions:

1. What different ways can you think of to categorise costs?

   - By function
   - By department
   - CapEx vs OpEx
   - Recurring vs non-recurring cost.
   - By behaviour

2. What is the definition of a variable cost?

   - A cost that increases proportionally with each unit of output

3. Give an example of a variable cost.

   - Raw materials, direct labour (direct labour is variable, despite the staff receiving a fixed salary per month. If output is increased by say 20%, then there will be more overtime, temporary labour or staff recruited. Likewise if output falls by 20%, then overtime will be cut, temps will be sent home and possibly staff will be laid off, so at category level, direct labour is variable)

4. Give an example of a fixed cost.

   - Rent, business rates, management salaries

5. Give an example of a semi-fixed/semi-variable cost.

   - Electricity, telephone

6. Draw a graph of a stepped cost.

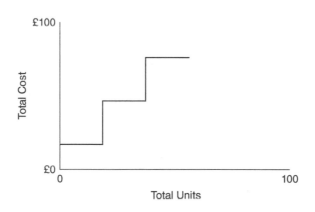

COST BEHAVIOUR

Costs behave in a number of different ways:

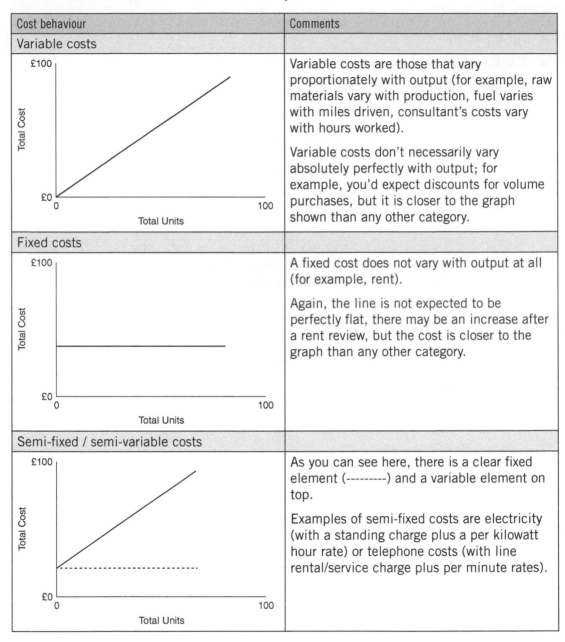

Cost behaviour	Comments
Variable costs	
	Variable costs are those that vary proportionately with output (for example, raw materials vary with production, fuel varies with miles driven, consultant's costs vary with hours worked).
	Variable costs don't necessarily vary absolutely perfectly with output; for example, you'd expect discounts for volume purchases, but it is closer to the graph shown than any other category.
Fixed costs	
	A fixed cost does not vary with output at all (for example, rent).
	Again, the line is not expected to be perfectly flat, there may be an increase after a rent review, but the cost is closer to the graph than any other category.
Semi-fixed / semi-variable costs	
	As you can see here, there is a clear fixed element (---------) and a variable element on top.
	Examples of semi-fixed costs are electricity (with a standing charge plus a per kilowatt hour rate) or telephone costs (with line rental/service charge plus per minute rates).

Cost behaviour	Comments
Stepped costs	
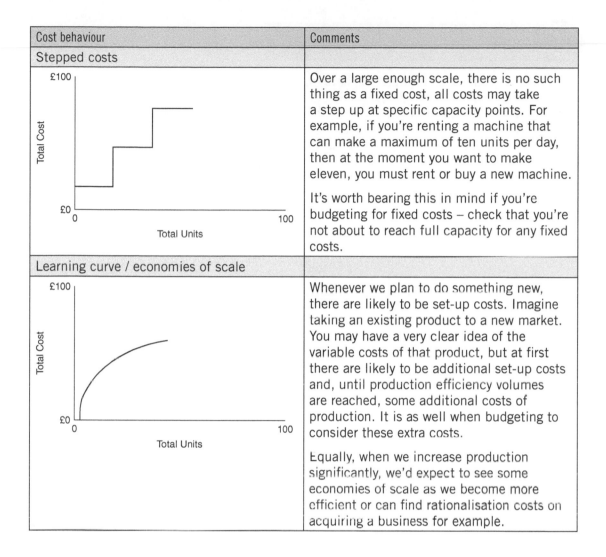	Over a large enough scale, there is no such thing as a fixed cost, all costs may take a step up at specific capacity points. For example, if you're renting a machine that can make a maximum of ten units per day, then at the moment you want to make eleven, you must rent or buy a new machine. It's worth bearing this in mind if you're budgeting for fixed costs – check that you're not about to reach full capacity for any fixed costs.
Learning curve / economies of scale	
	Whenever we plan to do something new, there are likely to be set-up costs. Imagine taking an existing product to a new market. You may have a very clear idea of the variable costs of that product, but at first there are likely to be additional set-up costs and, until production efficiency volumes are reached, some additional costs of production. It is as well when budgeting to consider these extra costs. Equally, when we increase production significantly, we'd expect to see some economies of scale as we become more efficient or can find rationalisation costs on acquiring a business for example.

🗣🗣 COACHING SESSION 14

Think of a recent car journey that you have made. It doesn't matter whether you were driving or a passenger. It doesn't matter if the journey cost you money (as the driver) or if it cost someone else money (as you were a passenger) or whether it cost your company money (if it was a business trip). Please calculate the cost per mile (or cost per kilometre) of that car journey here:

What costs did you include in the calculation?

- If you only included the cost of fuel and possibly parking, then you have used **Marginal Costing**.

   Marginal costing is when we count the cost of one more unit of output. Marginal costing is useful for decision making. If you were trying to decide whether to drive or whether to take public transport, then only the fuel (and parking) would be relevant.

Consequently when making business decisions, we only count the costs arising directly as a result of that decision.

If you were making a decision on whether to launch a new product, you would include any set-up costs, the cost of producing, distributing and marketing the new product, but you would not include a portion of the overheads from head office. Those costs will be incurred whether you launch the product or not!

■ If you included a portion of tax, insurance, depreciation (or lease costs), maintenance, etc., then you used **Absorption Costing**.

Absorption costing is when you include a portion of all the costs of running the business into each department and then into each unit of output.

Absorption costing is good for budgeting – we would want to cover all the costs of driving over the course of the year. It can also be good for pricing if you use a cost plus pricing model. Back to our driving / public transport decision; whilst we would decide whether to drive or not based on the marginal cost, we would charge our expenses out at the fully absorbed cost.

We might absorb overhead costs into units of production thus:

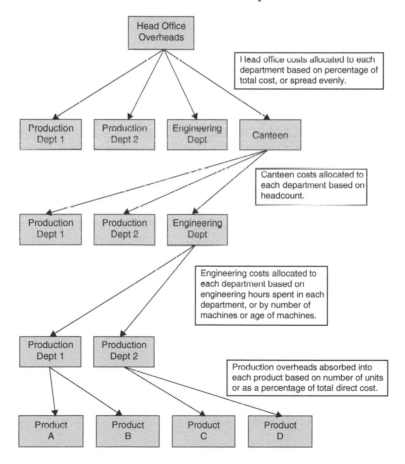

Thus each product carries the full cost of production plus a portion of all company overheads to give us a total cost per unit.

This can be used to ensure that the price we charge covers the total cost plus any required mark-up.

This can also be used to set a **Standard Cost** for each unit allowing us to produce budgets and targets for production managers based on a standard cost. Production managers can then focus on managing production volumes rather than worrying about procurement price rises outside of their control.

NEXT STEPS

In this section you have:

- Understood how costs can be categorised and how they behave
- Understood three costing methods:
  - marginal costing (for decision making)
  - absorption costing (for budgeting)
  - standard costing (for control)

In the next section we will look in more detail at budgeting.

TAKEAWAYS

This is your opportunity to take stock of what you've learned from this chapter. You might now want to choose other chapters and exercises to focus on, or you can continue to work through the whole book if this better fits your needs.

1. How and when does your company use marginal costing? What examples of company marginal cost decisions can you review?

_____

_____

_____

_____

_____

_____

_____

_____

_____

2. How does your company allocate and absorb different categories of overheads?

_____

_____

_____

_____

_____

_____

_____

_____

_____

3. Does your company produce management accounts using standard costs? How would this help with management control?

_____

_____

_____

_____

_____

_____

_____

_____

_____

9

HOW DO I PUT A BUDGET TOGETHER?

✔ OUTCOMES FROM THIS CHAPTER

- In this chapter we will:
  - Review a seven step budgeting process
  - Look at some tips for producing achievable budgets linked to overall company objectives.

COACHING SESSION 15

What are the benefits of budgeting?	What are the drawbacks or difficulties of budgeting?

SUGGESTED SOLUTION TO COACHING SESSION 15

Benefits of budgeting:	Drawbacks or difficulties of budgeting:
• To plan to achieve company objectives and targets	• Time consuming
• To control income, expenditure and cash flow	• Restrictive
• To allocate resources appropriately to achieve objectives	• Things change during the year but budgeted targets are still in place
• To prioritise activities	• De-motivating if not involved in the process, if budgets seem unachievable or if they're cut later
• To communicate objectives and targets to all levels of staff in the organisation	
• To motivate staff to reach challenging but achievable targets	

TOP-DOWN / BOTTOM-UP BUDGETING

Most organisations will carry out a mix of top-down and bottom-up budgeting where senior managers will set some very top level targets (revenue, costs and margins) for each department, but then departmental managers produce more detailed plans. The trick is to negotiate to ensure the bottom-up budgets fall in line with top-down expectations but are still achievable.

MOST COMMON MISTAKES IN BUDGETING

Some of the most common mistakes in budgeting include:

- Padding the budget before submission, to mitigate any cuts.
    - Padding the budget just leads to cuts, then greater padding, then greater cuts. It adds time to the process and it doesn't build trust with your senior manager or finance business partner.
- Budgeting incrementally (last year's 'actuals' plus a bit).
    - This leads to wanting to spend your whole budget, or you won't get as much next year and so there is no incentive to achieve efficiency savings.
    - If you ever need much more budget, to complete a special project for example, it will be very difficult to justify.

- Over time, you will forget the assumptions in the original budget. If you only budget for last year plus a few tweaks, when you receive your monthly reports, how will you know the reasons for the variances?

  - Presenting an incremental budget leads to a line-by-line review of every single income and cost item by the finance department, requiring a justification for every item. This may be difficult if you've forgotten the original assumptions.

- Budgeting as though everything is stable.

  - If you don't understand what the company is trying to achieve overall, how will you know what is required of your department?

- Ignoring risks.

  - It is perfectly valid to include some contingency figures in the budget for any identified risks. However, just adding say 10% to the costs is likely to lead to your contingency budget being cut.

- Budgeting on your own.

  - It will be much easier to think of everything if you work in a team with everyone involved and brainstorm all the things you need to cover in your budget.

BUDGET PROCESS

When budgeting, it's a good idea to follow a process to organise your thoughts. This will help you to put your budget together, but it also provides a structure to present your budget and will put you in a good negotiating position to ensure your budget is approved and achievable.

Many managers will produce budgets based on the previous year's actual income and costs with a few tweaks. Very often managers will be tempted to 'pad' their budget in preparation of their budget being cut. This leads to long-winded iterative budget processes where budgets are padded, then cut by increasing amounts each year.

Instead, let's review a robust process that will help you to link your budget to the organisation's strategic aims to put you in a better negotiating position from the start.

Step		Notes	Example
1	Objectives	Start with the overall strategic objectives of the organisation. Now consider what your division, department or business unit needs to do to support the overall strategic aims.	Let's say you're a professional institute and your objective is to double membership in five years. You currently have 120,000 members and the training process for new members takes three years. You currently train around 3,000 students a year.
2	Limiting factor	Step two is to identify what will stop you achieving your objectives (these are your limiting factors). It's important to understand what bottlenecks stand in the way of achieving your objectives; these will need to be overcome. Planning for this will help you to put your budget together. There may be more than one limiting factor. You will need to run through and plan for each.	What will stop you from doubling membership? Student numbers will probably be the main limiting factor. How many graduates will want to train in your profession? Your options are: ■ Increase recruitment efforts. ■ Recruit students from other institutes. ■ Give reciprocal membership to overseas institutes. ■ Acquire or merge with another institute.
3	First part of your budget	The next step is to put together a zero based budget for the critical plans you've put in place for overcoming your limiting factors. **Zero Based Budgeting** involves starting with a blank sheet of paper: ■ What do we need to do? ■ How will we do it? ■ What resources do we need? ■ Therefore what will it cost?	Will any one of the options fulfil your objectives, or will you need to implement a mix of options or all options? Put plans in place on how you will go about this and budget accordingly. What are your operational plans? What resources will you need? What will this cost and what income will this bring in?
4	The rest of your budget	The rest of your budget should just fall out of your existing plans. This can be done on a more **'incremental'** basis (i.e. based on historical information). We should, however, still review what efficiency savings could be made.	Once you know how many students you'll attract, you will know how many registrations, how many sets of learning materials, how many exam places, etc. that you will need. Budget for all steps of your operational process.

5	Present and negotiate your budget	In presenting your budget, use the same process: ■ Slide one reminds them of the overall objectives for your five year plan and the objectives for this year. ■ Slide two shows what your division, department or business unit needs to do to support the organisation's strategic aims. ■ Slide three describes how you will achieve your objectives, what you will do, therefore what resources you will need, and thus what will be the incomes and costs. ■ Only then should you present the detail of the budget numbers.	If your senior managers or finance department challenge your budget, you can now review the objectives and your plans. Discuss and agree if any of your plans can be delayed, or changed, without affecting the objectives.
6	Agree the budget	Finalise your agreed budget.	
7	Monitor and review	Each month, check progress on your operational plans – are you achieving against your timelines and review your budget. Are you on track? If not, what can you do to get back to budget?	The benefit of this process is that you have stated your objectives and assumptions at each stage. Consequently, each month it should be easy to spot the reasons for any variances as you will know what you've done differently from your budget assumptions.

COACHING SESSION 16

Now work through the budgeting process to produce your budget:

Step		Notes	Your budget workings:
1	Objectives	Start with the overall strategic objectives of the organisation. Now consider what your division, department or business unit needs to do to support the overall strategic aims.	

2	Limiting factor	Step two is to identify what will stop you achieving your objectives (these are your limiting factors). There may be more than one limiting factor, you will need to run through and plan for each.	
3	First part of your budget	The next step is to put together a zero based budget for the critical plans you've put in place for overcoming your limiting factors. What do we need to do? How will we do it? What resources do we need? What will it cost?	
4	The rest of your budget	The rest of your budget should just fall out of your existing plans. This can be done on a more 'Incremental' basis (i.e. based on historical information). What efficiency savings could be made?	
5	Present and negotiate your budget	Prepare your presentation. Slide one: overall objectives for five year plan. Slide two: your department's objectives to support these. Slide three: ■ What will you do? ■ How will you do it? ■ What resources do you need? ■ What will it cost? Separate handout: detailed budget numbers.	

ONLINE RESOURCE

A downloadable budgeting template is available at:

www.TYCoachbooks.com/Finance

We have not considered any risks to your budget here. If you feel that there are significant risks of unforeseen events occurring, take a look at the risk budgeting section in chapter 14: Specifics for Project Managers to help you to produce a defensible contingency budget.

Here is an example budgeting spreadsheet that you can use to complete the detailed costings:

Annual Budget

Description	Time											
	January	February	March	April	May	June	July	August	September	October	November	December
Income												
Total Income												
Expenditure												
Total Expenditure												
Net Profit												

ONLINE RESOURCE

A downloadable budgeting spreadsheet is available at:

www.TYCoachbooks.com/Finance

NEXT STEPS

In this section you have:

- Reviewed a budgeting process
- Completed a budget template
- Considered the best approach to presenting your budget

In the next section we will look in more detail at managing your budget; understanding variances and controlling costs.

 TAKEAWAYS

This is your opportunity to take stock of what you've learned from this chapter. You might now want to choose other chapters and exercises to focus on, or you can continue to work through the whole book if this better fits your needs.

1. What are your organisation's key strategic objectives?

_____

_____

_____

_____

_____

_____

_____

_____

2. What would you need to do in your department, division or business unit to support these objectives?

_____

_____

_____

_____

_____

_____

_____

_____

3. Who did you present your budget to? What was their feedback?

_____

_____

_____

_____

_____

_____

_____

_____

4. What have you learned for next time?

_____

_____

_____

_____

_____

_____

_____

_____

_____

_____

10 WHAT'S NEXT – HOW DO I MANAGE MY BUDGET?

 OUTCOMES FROM THIS CHAPTER

- In this chapter we will look
    - Typical monthly report formats, review possible reasons for variances, and ways to improve financial results.
    - We will also look at why businesses have to re-forecast.

MANAGING YOUR BUDGET

Assuming you've put together your budget using the process outlined in the last chapter, when you receive your first month's management accounts, you will already know what all the variances will be and understand the reasons for them, because you know what you assumed in your budget, and you know what has happened differently. However, sometimes we find ourselves in a new role in a new department or business, responsible for a budget compiled by the previous manager.

Imagine the situation where you are a new manager in an Oodgit Manufacturing Plant. Days after joining the company, you are sent the latest monthly report.

What may have caused the variances?

- What questions do you need to ask?

- What do you suggest to improve results next month?

First, let's look at the format of the management accounts:

Down the left hand side we have a typical Income Statement format and across the top we have columns for a standard cost, the budget for the month, the actual for the month and the variance (difference between budget and actual) as well as the variance percentage (the variance as a percentage of the budget).

Oodgit manufacturing management report

	Unit cost @ standard	April			
		Budget	Actual	Variance	Vari %
Units		400,000	300,000	−100,000	−25%
		£	£	£	
Sales	0.800	320,000	240,000	80,000	−25%
Raw Materials	0.030	12,000	8,400	3,600	30%
Direct Labour	0.020	8,000	7,750	250	3%
Variable Overheads	0.020	8,000	6,000	2,000	25%
Gross Profit	**0.730**	**292,000**	**217,850**	**−74,150**	**−25%**
Gross Margin	**91%**	**91%**	**91%**		
Overheads					
Distribution	0.12	48,000	36,000	12,000	25%
Marketing	0.07	28,000	14,000	14,000	50%
Rent	0.08	32,000	32,000	0	0%
Electricity	0.08	32,000	31,000	1,000	3%
Management Salaries	0.10	40,000	40,000	0	0%
Engineering	0.05	20,000	20,000	0	0%
Admin	0.02	8,000	8,000	0	0%
Operating Profit	**0.29**	**84,000**	**36,850**	**−47,150**	**−56%**
Operating Margin	**36%**	**26%**	**15%**		

COACH'S TIP

All variances are shown as negative (−) if they are adverse (worse than budgeted) or positive (+) if they are favourable (better than budgeted).

Typically we would also see a '**year to date**' section to the right, so that we can see the trend too. Sometimes we may also see a re-forecast section (if new forecasts are made regularly).

🗨🗨 COACHING SESSION 17

Let's review each line in turn.

1. The first line item isn't monetary, it is the units produced. As you can see, volumes are down by 25%. We'd want to ask our marketing and production managers if they can explain this, but for now let's continue on with the rest of the report.

2. The sales income is also less than budgeted. Typically there are two main reasons for a sales variance: volume (we made more or fewer units than planned) or price (we charged more or less per unit than planned).

Question: Is this variance due to volume, price or a mix of the two?

3. The materials' costs are also less than budgeted. The main reasons for a materials variance are: volume (we made more or fewer units than planned) or price (we bought cheaper or more expensive materials than planned).

Question: Is this variance due to volume, price or a mix of the two?

There are other possible reasons for materials' variances:

- Mix (using a different mix of products) – for example a food manufacturer may choose to use NutraSweet® instead of sugar

- Yield (achieving a better yield) – for example a drinks manufacturer may manage to fill cans at exactly 330ml (instead of the planned 335ml to ensure there are no 'low-fills')

- Wastage (more or less waste or more or fewer defects than expected)

4. Direct labour is less than budgeted, but nowhere near as low as we'd expect from the volume. Whilst it is unlikely that we'd be able to save the full 25% on labour (it would be tricky to manage staff, overtime, temps, etc. to achieve the full 25% saving), 3% seems very low. The main reasons for labour variances are: volume (we made more or fewer units than planned), price (we paid more or less per hour), efficiency (people worked harder or less hard than planned), idle time (staff had to wait around for production to start).

Question: What do you believe is the reason for this variance?

5. Variable overheads are exactly 25% down on budget.

Question: How do you explain this?

6. Let's suppose you haven't been to the warehouse yet.

Question: From the figures shown, do you think that we have a warehouse, warehousemen, delivery drivers and trucks of our own, or do we outsource distribution to a specialist logistics firm and pay a fixed rate per box delivered?

7. Marketing costs are exactly 50% down on budget.

Question: Can you think of any links between this variance and any others in the report?

8. A 3% saving has been made on electricity costs.

Question: Can you think of any reasons for this?

9. We'll ignore the engineering, management salaries, admin and rent line items as there are no variances here.

10. A key point to note is that the gross margin is roughly on budget, but there is an 11 point reduction in operating profit margin.

Question: Why would there be such an effect on operating margin, if not on gross margin?

SUGGESTED SOLUTIONS TO COACHING SESSION 17

Q. No.	Answer
2	The sales variance is clearly due to volume; it is the same percentage variance as the units line above.
3	The materials variance is mostly down to volume, but there is a price variance in there too. If it were just volume, the variance would be 25%, the same as the units. In this case there is an additional 5% saving that must be due to price.
4	Initially we may think that the labour variance could be due to downtime.
	This would make sense as it would explain why production was down, maybe the machines were broken for a while. However, it is unlikely to be due to downtime in this example. If we look further down the report, we see that engineering costs are on budget, whereas we'd be likely to spend more on subcontractors, spare parts, etc. if the machines were broken.
	This leaves the main reason likely for the variance as efficiency. A possible reason for this could be linked to the materials variance. If the materials bought were so much cheaper than planned, maybe they are not of the same quality either – leading to lots of rework or just difficulty in making the components fit. This would explain why we'd not managed to save more on labour given the drop in volume.
5	From what we know about absorption costing (see chapter 7) and accruals (see chapter 2), we know that overheads will be accrued for on the basis of a standard cost of 2p per unit. Consequently the variance is bound to be 25%, however, we probably haven't received all the invoices yet. Once these have been received, we may find that next month shows an adverse variance. This is a key point to remember when reviewing your monthly reports – what is a real actual cost and what has been accrued?
6	The distribution costs are exactly 25% down on budget, so it is likely that we outsource distribution. If we had our own warehouse and delivery team we would likely make much less of a saving, as all the drivers would still be going out to all the customers but with less full trucks saving us almost nothing.
7	It is likely that a cut in marketing costs may have led to the reduction in sales. However, it is possible that there is some other reason for the reduction in sales (e.g. we never sell many oodgits when it's raining) and given this information, we decided to delay marketing spend until things (the weather) improve.

8	There's no doubt that the reduced production will have had an impact on electricity costs. However, we should ask ourselves whether 3% was to be expected. Analysis may show that we'd expect to save maybe 10%, this would then alert us to more variances (for example a price rise in electricity costs). It would be important to find this out as early as possible as we might be able to find other areas to make savings that would offset some of this price rise. If we didn't look deeper at the electricity variance, assuming that it was all down to the reduced production, it would be another month before we discovered the price rise, and another month would have gone by with no cost-cutting action to offset it!
10	The operating margin has been affected so badly because there is a high level of fixed costs in this business. When volume is reduced, the variable (direct) costs fall more or less in line. However, any business with high levels of fixed costs will suffer disproportionate reductions in operating profit when volume falls as it is difficult to make savings against fixed costs.

 COACH'S TIP

When reviewing management accounts with your finance business partner, or in management meetings, it would be useful to:

- Get sight of the reports prior to the meeting.

- Review the total variance at the bottom line, then trace up the variances column looking for the biggest variances contributing to the overall variance.

- See if you can understand the reasons for the main variances. If you can't, then ask questions of your finance business partner.

It is quite common that when finance are presenting the figures in management meetings very few questions are asked. Maybe you believe that most people understand what is being presented, but ask yourself this; if you struggle to keep up with the presentation, is it possible that everyone is struggling to keep up? There is a good chance that if you ask a few questions, this will slow the presentation down and everyone will be better able to take in the information.

WHAT'S WITH ALL THE RE-FORECASTING?

COACHING SESSION 18

What is the purpose of re-forecasting? What are the benefits?

SUGGESTED SOLUTION TO COACHING SESSION 18

- Re-forecasting can help us to control our costs against a more accurate re-forecast than sticking with the budget does, as things change in the outside world making our original budget unrealistic.

- As we work through the year, we can include our actual costs-to-date along with re-forecasted figures for the remainder of the year to help us to plan what is required to achieve our original budgeted targets.

- In a public company, (plc in the UK, Inc. in the US) it is important to communicate high level forecasted figures to the shareholders to prepare them for any changes in expected performance.

In any company, the owners or directors will need to understand the changing conditions of the market and the impact on results: will they achieve their targets and will they have enough cash to continue operations, etc.?

Just like budgeting, re-forecasting is difficult. Although the actual results to date are known, there is still considerable uncertainty in future results.

For a public company, communicating the forecast is critical to the share price. If a company can accurately forecast and communicate this, the share price will reflect the new forecast, but will move less than if forecasts are not achieved.

Consider these examples:

- A company noticing a change in the market place re forecasts accordingly for lower profits than originally budgeted. The share price falls slightly initially, but at year end – when the forecast is achieved – the share price will remain stable or maybe rise slightly in appreciation of the control shown.

- A company constantly reaffirms that their budget will be achieved, but late in the year issues a profit warning, or fails to achieve their budget with no warning. The share price will likely fall considerably: partly due to the fall in profits, but additionally for the lack of control and lack of credibility of the management.

- A company constantly re-forecasts on budget, but then at year end achieves much better results than forecasted. Chances are that the share price could fall despite the improved performance! Again, the lack of understanding of the business and lack of control have a negative impact.

Budget holders within any business may be required to re-forecast regularly (half-yearly, quarterly or, in very volatile businesses, perhaps even monthly).

Re-forecasting is an opportunity to discuss with your senior managers and finance business partners the changing state of the market and your estimation of the impacts and actions you could take to achieve your targets. It is also an opportunity to ask for help if things are changing for the worse and you feel you cannot achieve your original targets.

Unfortunately in many businesses, because of cultural issues, budget holders may feel that their re-forecast must come back to the original budget no matter what has changed. This is a mistake, if all managers re-forecast back to budget, the exercise fulfils no purpose but only wastes everyone's time! The impact (as seen in the above example) could be that communications to shareholders mislead them and by year end the impact on the share price could be significant.

COACH'S TIP

Whenever budgeting or re-forecasting (or indeed putting together any investment proposal) it is a good idea to produce forecasts for three scenarios:

1   The most likely scenario. This is the forecast that you will work to and submit to finance . You can't submit three versions of the budget, so this is the one you use. The others are realistic plans that you can move to if things change.

2   The optimistic scenario. This scenario includes all your plans for if things go horribly well. It is not just an optimistic view, it is a realistic plan for how to operate if, for example, sales are better than expected. How will you cope with the capacity requirements? Maybe you need to have plans in place with outsourced resources. It is a plan that you can implement quickly as soon as you notice an increase in sales.

3   The pessimistic scenario. What could go wrong? This plan includes the most likely risks along with your plans for how to deal with these risks as they occur. You might also include other cost-cutting plans you would be able to implement to offset any overspends elsewhere in your budget.

NEXT STEPS

In this section you have:

- Reviewed a set of management accounts

- Understood reasons for some common variances

- Understood the 'story' that the management accounts are telling you

- Understood the importance of re-forecasting accurately

- Reviewed the three scenario approach to budgeting and re-forecasting

In the next section we will review how to gain approval for investment ideas and projects

TAKEAWAYS

This is your opportunity to take stock of what you've learned from this chapter. You might now want to choose other chapters and exercises to focus on, or you can continue to work through the whole book if this better fits your needs.

1. Where can you get a copy of your department / division / business unit monthly management accounts?

_____

_____

_____

_____

_____

_____

_____

_____

2. What are the key things you learned from your monthly reports?

_____

_____

_____

_____

_____

_____

_____

_____

_____

3. What actions could you take personally to improve your department / division / business unit financial results?

_____

_____

_____

_____

_____

_____

_____

_____

_____

4. Who else would benefit from being involved in the monthly management review or re-forecasting process?

_____

_____

_____

_____

_____

_____

_____

_____

_____

HOW DO I KNOW THAT MY GREAT IDEA WILL PAY OFF?

 OUTCOMES FROM THIS CHAPTER

- In this chapter we will:
  - Review break-even analysis as a tool for establishing what level of output is required to break-even or to make a profit.

Self-test quiz:

1. What three lines will you need to draw to produce a break-even chart?

   -
   -
   -

2. Which two lines cross to give us the break-even?

   -
   -

3. What is the formula for break-even?

   -

4. How would you amend the formula to achieve a targeted profit figure?

   -

5. What is the name given to the difference between your planned output and the break-even output?

   -

Suggested solutions:

1. What three lines will you need to draw to produce a break-even chart?
   - Fixed costs
   - Total costs
   - Total revenue

2. Which two lines cross to give us the break-even?
   - Total costs
   - Total revenue

3. What is the formula for break-even?
   - Fixed costs ÷ contribution per unit

4. How would you amend the formula to achieve a targeted profit figure?
   - (fixed costs + target profit) ÷ contribution per unit

5. What is the name given to the difference between your planned output and the break-even output?
   - Margin of safety

Break-even analysis is a method for determining whether a new product or service or launching an existing product or service into a new market will cover its costs, or preferably make a profit.

This method isn't good for evaluating projects that require an up-front investment (see the next chapter for help with projects involving some initial development).

Let's look at an example now:

Imagine you are an entrepreneur thinking of launching a new product. You've done all your planning and discovered that:

- Renting premises will cost £1,000 per month
- Hiring staff will cost £2,000 per month
- Leasing machinery will cost £1,000 per month
- Raw materials will cost you £7 per unit

You've also done some market research, the results of which show that you can sell 400 units per month at a price of £25.

First we'll need to plot the fixed costs (see chapter 8 for more information on costing), the rent, staff and machinery (£4,000 total).

Next, we'll plot the variable costs (see chapter 8), the costs of production, i.e. raw materials (£7 per unit). If we plot these on top of the fixed costs, then it will actually show the total cost at each level of production and sales.

And then finally, we need to plot the selling price, £25 per unit:

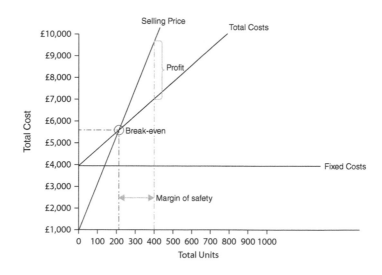

The point at which the total sales income (selling price) is equal to the total costs is the break-even point. Simply draw a line from the break-even point to the number of units and we can see that we break-even at 220 units.

In addition, we can compare the break-even units to the market prediction of being able to sell 400 units per month. The difference between the break-even units and the marketing prediction is known as the **margin of safety**. The greater the margin of safety, the more we can afford demand to fall without slipping into a loss making position. We can also see the level of profit we would achieve if we manage to sell the expected 400 units.

One really useful point about graphing the break-even is that if we need to change our plans in any way, we can see the impact of this on the break-even point (this is known as sensitivity analysis).

Imagine a situation where you were able to reduce the fixed costs, as you can see, the break-even moves backwards to around 160 units:

Now imagine a situation where you are able to reduce the variable cost per unit: Again, the break-even point falls back, this time to just under 200 units.

Finally, let's change the selling price:

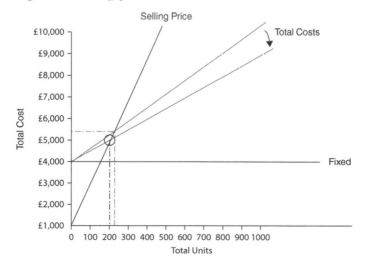

This time the break-even point moves to around 400 units.

Remember, if you change the selling price, this may affect the volume that you can sell, so you would have to do more market research.

Whilst it is helpful for our understanding of break-even to view a break-even graph, it is more convenient to calculate break-even using a formula. The original break-even example is calculated here:

$$\text{Break-even} = \frac{\text{Fixed Costs}}{\text{Contribution per Unit*}} \qquad \frac{£4,000}{£18^*} = 220 \text{ units}$$

*Where Contribution per Unit equals:

+ Selling Price   £25

− Variable Costs   (£7)

= Contribution per Unit   £18

COACHING SESSION 19

If you have a new product to launch, or are launching an existing product into a new market, list the total fixed costs, variable costs and selling price here, then calculate your break-even point:

Fixed Costs:	£
Variable Costs per Unit:	£
Selling Price:	£
Contribution per Unit: + Selling Price − Variable Costs = Contribution per Unit	£

Now calculate your break-even here:

$$\frac{\text{Total Fixed Cost}}{\text{Contribution per Unit}} = \text{———} = \qquad \text{units}$$

NEXT STEPS

In this section you have:

- Understood and practised calculating a break-even point
- Understood sensitivity analysis applied to a break-even calculation

In the next section, we will review how to gain approval for investment ideas and projects requiring an up-front investment.

TAKEAWAYS

This is your opportunity to take stock of what you've learned from this chapter. You might now want to choose other chapters and exercises to focus on, or you can continue to work through the whole book if this better fits your needs.

1. Does your product or new market idea break-even?

_____

_____

_____

_____

_____

_____

_____

_____

_____

2. What profit do you anticipate your product or market bringing?

_____

_____

_____

_____

_____

_____

_____

_____

_____

3. What actions could you take to improve this result?

4. What have you learned for next time?

12 HOW DO I GET FINANCE TO APPROVE MY GREAT IDEA?

 OUTCOMES FROM THIS CHAPTER

- In this chapter we will look at:
  - A number of financial evaluation techniques for decision making
  - Pros and cons for each technique
  - Which to use in different situations

Self-test quiz:

1. Describe the Benefit:Cost ratio.

   ■

2. Describe the Payback Period calculation.

   ■

3. What does NPV stand for?

   ■

4. Define NPV.

   ■

5. What is the Discount Factor?

   ■

6. What is IRR?

   ■

Suggested solutions:

1. Describe the Benefit:Cost ratio.

   ■ It's the ratio between total benefits and total costs. If total benefits exceed total costs, the project is approved

2. Describe the Payback Period calculation.

   ■ It's a time-based measure showing how long in years it takes for the net cash inflows to equal the up-front investment

3. What does NPV stand for?

   ■ Net Present Value

4. Define NPV.

   ■ NPV is the sum of all future cash flows stated in today's money terms. A project with a positive NPV should be approved

5. What is the Discount Factor?

   ■ A discount factor is the percentage we use to discount future cash flows, it is based on the Weighted Average Cost of Capital (WACC)

6. What is IRR?

   ■ Internal Rate of Return is the break-even cost of capital at which the NPV of a project will = 0

So, you have a great idea. Now it's time to persuade others – is the opportunity worth it financially?

First there are some things we need to consider in terms of what costs and incomes or savings we should include. For this we can use the acronym '**RICH**':

R   Relevant – costs and incomes included in the financial evaluation must be relevant. Any costs that have already been spent are now 'sunk' costs and therefore irrelevant and not to be included. For example, imagine you have already spent £15,000 on some market research and now you're ready to make an informed decision. The £15,000 is spent and cannot be 'un-spent', it is irrelevant to your decision now. You should disregard this cost in your calculations.

I   Incremental – costs and incomes included in the financial evaluation must be incurred as a direct result of the decision. If you are looking to run this new project from your current office, there is no need to include allocated overheads (such as rent of the building, utilities, etc.) in the calculation. These costs will be incurred whether you decide to proceed with the opportunity or not. However, if there is no room for the new project team in the existing office and you will use a Portakabin hired specially, then the costs of this must be included.

C   Cash – costs and incomes must be counted when the cash actually flows, rather than on the profit or accruals basis. The profits from your opportunity may look really good, but if all the cash inflows happen at the end of the project, there is a time cost of money and in real cash terms this may affect your decision.

H   Holistic – costs and incomes arising from the project must be included. Say for example that you are getting some 'free' resource; a secondee from another department. Whilst this is a free resource for your project, if the secondee is being replaced by a temporary employee in their normal job, this is a cost of running the project. Take into account costs incurred anywhere in the business for this evaluation.

The first thing we need to do is put together a cash flow forecast for the opportunity. Take account of all cash flows into and out of the business when the cash actually moves. Take into account any up-front investment used to get the project started in time 0, then count all other costs and incomes in the relevant years that the cash flows (in times 1–10) in the following template:

Financial evaluation of business opportunity		
Ratio	Project A	Project B
Benefit:Cost ratio	70:50	130:50
If you then divide both sides by the up-front investment, you can see the ratio as ?:1	1.4:1	2.6:1
Or we can express this as a percentage of benefits over costs	40%	160%

ONLINE RESOURCE

A downloadable cash flow forecasting spreadsheet is available at:

www.TYCoachbooks.com/Finance

There are five different methods of financially evaluating projects. We'll look at all of them here because different businesses and investors will be interested in different tools. We'll also review the benefits and drawbacks of each.

Firstly, let's use a comparison of two different projects in order to compare the methods. The two projects both involve an up-front investment of £50,000. Project A only lasts for two years and thereafter there are no further cash flows. Project B lasts for five years.

For this example we have summarised the cash flows into a single stream, the total of all cash inflows and cash outflows for each time period (the total figures at the bottom of the chart available for download). As you can see, the two projects last for different time periods, which makes the comparison even more complex.

Time	Project A	Project B
0	−50,000	−50,000
1	35,000	20,000
2	35,000	20,000
3		20,000
4		30,000
5		40,000

BENEFIT:COST ANALYSIS

The first method we will examine is the Benefit:Cost ratio. In order to calculate this ratio, we simply add up all the up-front costs and compare them to the net cash inflows over the life of the project:

Benefit:Cost ratio	70:50	130:50
If you then divide both sides by the up-front investment, you can see the ratio as ?:1	1.4:1	2.6:1
Or we can express this as a percentage of benefits over costs	40%	160%

There is no formal agreement on how the Benefit:Cost ratio is displayed, so any of the three formats is acceptable.

If the benefit exceeds the cost, then the project is accepted.

Benefits

The method is very simple to calculate and to communicate.

Drawbacks

Since this method takes no account of when the cash flows, it may lead you to accept a project where all the cash inflows are at the end of a project – by which time your business may have gone into liquidation! For longer term investments, this is not a good tool.

Why would you use this method?

For very short term projects, this method is fine and no further analysis is needed. If the benefits exceed the costs within two to three years, then it can be considered a 'no-brainer'.

PAYBACK PERIOD

The next method we will look at is the payback period method. This is a time-based method that simply looks at how long in time it takes for the cash inflows to equal the cash outflows (i.e. for the project to break-even). For our example above the payback periods are:

	Project A	Project B
Calculation	The initial investment is £50k. ■ Year 1: net cash inflow of £35k. ■ Year 2: net cash inflow of £35k	The initial investment is £50k. Cash inflows by year are: 1=£20k 2=£20k 3=£20k 4=£30k 5=£40k
Payback period	In year 2	In year 3

If the payback period is less than the company's target, then the project is accepted.

Benefits

This method is really simple to calculate and to communicate.

The method drives us to be concerned with cash flow; we accept projects that pay back more quickly and we'll have cash coming in early that we can re-invest into other projects.

To some extent, the method takes account of risk. When forecasting the cash flows of a project, which figures are more accurate: the first years or the later years? Of course the earlier years are likely to be more certain – the longer a project goes on the more risks that may occur, so the cash flow forecasts of later years are less certain. The payback method drives us to choose projects that pay back quickly and so we can eliminate later, riskier cash flows from our decision.

Drawbacks

This method is short sighted, in that we ignore cash flows after the payback period. The two projects above are difficult to choose between intuitively. However, if project B actually lasted for ten years and the cash flows grew every year from year six to year ten, intuitively we might think project B is better. But the payback period method would ignore this and still drive us to choose project A.

Why would you use this method?

This is a quick and simple method to calculate and will give you a good rule of thumb; if the project pays back in a few short years, then it will be of interest and we may use some more sophisticated methods to analyse further.

The types of company that tend to rely more heavily on this method are those that are either a) risk averse (and so prefer to generate cash flows quickly before any risks occur) or b) have limited access to capital and so require projects to pay back quickly in order to fund future projects.

RETURN ON INVESTMENT / ACCOUNTING RATE OF RETURN

The next method we will look at is Return on Investment (ROI), although there is no agreed defined calculation for ROI. If someone asks to see a return on investment calculation, they may want to see any or all of the methods shown in this section, or maybe they are looking for the Accounting Rate of Return (ARR) method. This is the method we'll explain now. This method normally uses average annual profits (as opposed to cash flows) expressed as a percentage of the initial investment. Here we will use the cash flow as this is a more appropriate under our RICH rules listed above.

Method: $\dfrac{\text{Average annual profit}}{\text{Initial investment} \times 100}$	Project A	Project B
Accounting Rate of return	$\dfrac{35{,}000 \times 100}{50{,}0000} = 70\%$	$\dfrac{26{,}000 \times 100}{50{,}0000} = 52\%$

If the accounting rate of return is higher than the company's target, then the project is accepted.

Benefits

This method is really simple to calculate and to communicate and most people conceptually like the idea of a percentage return; it fits with a comparison of the company's total Return on Capital Employed (ROCE) or even a comparison with the interest rate that you could achieve by leaving the money invested instead.

Drawbacks

This is not a good method for decision making.

- Firstly we use average annual profits when our rule was to use cash. (In my example, I used cash for simplicity rather than calculating the profit by depreciating the up-front investment over the life of the project).

- Secondly it averages out the profits further. In our discussion on payback we said that later cash flows may be more risky, but this method has smoothed the lumpy cash flows into an average annual figure, thereby negating some of the risk that we project cash flows will start small and grow in later years!

Why would you use this method?

If the project's ARR is greater than the company's existing ROCE, then it would appear that the project will improve the company's results over the life of the project.

Take the results with a pinch of salt though! Take a look at the following example:

Time	Project C	Project D
0	−10,000	−10,000
1	4,000	4,000
2	4,000	4,000
3		4,000
4		4,000
5		4,000
ARR	40%	40%

Whilst both projects seem to give an accounting rate of return of 40%, the first project doesn't even pay back. This method can be quite misleading.

NET PRESENT VALUE (NPV)

Net present value is by far the best method for evaluating longer term projects, business plans and anything that requires a larger investment in the early stages. The reason is that it uses cash flows (unlike ARR), it takes account of the complete project life (unlike the payback period) and it takes account of the time value of money (unlike the Benefit:Cost ratio).

What do we mean by 'time value of money'? Would you rather be given £100 today, or £100 in a year's time? Clearly you'd want the money now. If you wanted to spend the money, what you could buy today with £100 is probably more than you could buy in one year from today because of *inflation*. In addition, if you wanted to invest your £100, it would be worth more than £100 in one year from today because of *interest*. The effect of interest and inflation means that money is worth more today than in the future.

Say we could invest our £100 today at a 10% interest rate, in one year from today it would be worth £110. In our example, we don't have cash today. We have cash flowing in over the next few years. If we had £110 arriving one year from today, what would it be worth in today's money? This is the process we're going to use now.

Looking at project A, one year from today we have £35,000 flowing in. What is that worth in today's values? Assuming a cost of capital (the cost to us of interest or dividends of using money invested in our business) of 10%, we'll discount the future cash flows from each project to state them in today's values. This is the method we'll use now:

Time	Discount Factor @ 10%	Project A		Project B	
		Cash Flow	Discounted Cash Flow	Cash Flow	Discounted Cash Flow
0	1	−50,000	−50,000	−50,000	−50,000
1	.909	35,000	31,815	20,000	18,180
2	.826	35,000	28,910	20,000	16,520
3	.751			20,000	15,020
4	.683			30,000	20,490
5	.621			40,000	24,840
NPV			10,725		45,050

We'll come back to the discount factor and explain how that is calculated shortly, but for now, just understand that money today (at time 0) is worth its face value, so the discount factor we use is 1. Simply multiply the £50,000 project A investment by the discount factor of 1. £50,000 today is worth £50,000 today.

But £35,000 flowing into the business in year 1 is worth a little less to us. Using a 10% discount rate, the discount factor for year 1 is 0.909. This simply means that £1 in a year's time is the equivalent of almost 91p today. If we invested 91p today at 10%, in a year's time we'd have £1.

Multiply the £35,000 flowing into the business in year 1 by 0.909 and we see that the discounted cash flow (i.e. the cash flow in today's values) is £31,815.

We continue to multiply all the actual cash flows by the discount factor to determine the discounted cash flow (the value of the actual cash flow in today's money terms).

The final step is to total up the discounted cash flow column.

Project A has an NPV of £10,725. This means that if we accept project A, we will have £10,725 more than if we do not implement project A. It is a positive value, so the project is worthwhile. However, Project B has a greater NPV, so it is the better project. The cash flows have been discounted, so even though the two projects have different lives, we can compare the two projects completely fairly.

If the NPV is greater than 0, then the project is accepted. When comparing projects, the greater the NPV the better.

Benefits

This method is the most reliable method as it:

- uses cash flows (unlike ARR)
- takes account of the complete project life (unlike the payback period)
- takes account of the time value of money (unlike the Benefit:Cost ratio).

Drawbacks

There are no real drawbacks. We do need to know (or estimate) the cost of capital. Whilst interest rates may fluctuate over time, we cannot wait for perfect information (or it will be too late, we'll have missed our opportunity) so it's not too important to estimate the cost of capital very accurately. Simply build in a little space for risk in the discount factor used, i.e. add a little to the real cost of capital to compensate for risk.

Why would you use this method?

The NPV tells you exactly how much cash *in today's values* you will have at the end of the time frame evaluated. As such this is a really good evaluation method.

COACH'S TIP

For the purposes of your business plan, you really only need to understand NPV conceptually, as you can download a spreadsheet at www.TYCoachbooks.com/Finance that will calculate all the evaluation results for you. However, we said we'd come back to the discount factor and also how to determine your cost of capital (i.e. what discount factor should we use?) So if you feel you need to understand this, we'll review it now:

The discount factor is calculated by the formula $1/(1+r)$, where r is the discount factor, so in our example where we used 10%, the formula is $1/1.1 = 0.909$. For year 2, we take $0.909/1.1 = 0.826$ and so on for each year. Or if you prefer $1/(1+r)^n$ where n is the number of the year you wish to calculate.

Below there is a table provided for you that lists all the discount factors for up to ten years at every cost of capital.

But more importantly, how do we determine the '**cost of capital**' that we wish to use? The cost of capital should strictly be the true cost of capital. The capital employed in your business is all the money invested by owners (total equity) plus long term loans (both of which you can pick up straight from the balance sheet) compared to the cost of this capital (all the interest paid on loans plus all the dividends paid). The cost of capital as a percentage of capital employed is your true cost of capital. However, most businesses will increase this for decision making purposes. For example if a company's true cost of capital is 6%, they may increase it to as much as 12%, partly to provide a buffer in case interest rates fluctuate, partly to encourage investment in projects that provide much more profit than just covering the cost of capital and finally to take account of risk. Higher discount factors will reduce much faster over time, so will discount the later, riskier cash flows more than lower discount factors.

If you're currently in business and putting together a business plan to gain approval for a project from your senior managers, then your finance department will be able to tell you exactly what discount factor to use. Alternative terms that your company may use for discount factor are: '**cost of capital**' or '**hurdle rate**'.

If you're an entrepreneur and putting together a business plan to start a completely new business, then either use the discount factor your funders favour, or take a middle of the road rate of around 12%. If the business is risky, you could also evaluate at 15% to test the sensitivity. If your business idea provides a positive NPV at 15%, it is quite impervious to risk. This might be quite persuasive for investors!

Discount table

Here is a table showing all the discount factors for up to ten years for each level of cost of capital:

Cost of capital	time 0	time 1	time 2	time 3	time 4	time 5	time 6	time 7	time 8	time 9	time 10
1%	1	0.9901	0.9803	0.9706	0.9610	0.9515	0.9420	0.9327	0.9235	0.9143	0.9053
2%	1	0.9804	0.9612	0.9423	0.9238	0.9057	0.8880	0.8706	0.8535	0.8368	0.8203
3%	1	0.9709	0.9426	0.9151	0.8885	0.8626	0.8375	0.8131	0.7894	0.7664	0.7441
4%	1	0.9615	0.9246	0.8890	0.8548	0.8219	0.7903	0.7599	0.7307	0.7026	0.6756
5%	1	0.9524	0.9070	0.8638	0.8227	0.7835	0.7462	0.7107	0.6768	0.6446	0.6139
6%	1	0.9434	0.8900	0.8396	0.7921	0.7473	0.7050	0.6651	0.6274	0.5919	0.5584
7%	1	0.9346	0.8734	0.8163	0.7629	0.7130	0.6663	0.6227	0.5820	0.5439	0.5083
8%	1	0.9259	0.8573	0.7938	0.7350	0.6806	0.6302	0.5835	0.5403	0.5002	0.4632
9%	1	0.9174	0.8417	0.7722	0.7084	0.6499	0.5963	0.5470	0.5019	0.4604	0.4224
10%	1	0.9091	0.8264	0.7513	0.6830	0.6209	0.5645	0.5132	0.4665	0.4241	0.3855
11%	1	0.9009	0.8116	0.7312	0.6587	0.5935	0.5346	0.4817	0.4339	0.3909	0.3522
12%	1	0.8929	0.7972	0.7118	0.6355	0.5674	0.5066	0.4523	0.4039	0.3606	0.3220
13%	1	0.8850	0.7831	0.6931	0.6133	0.5428	0.4803	0.4251	0.3762	0.3329	0.2946
14%	1	0.8772	0.7695	0.6750	0.5921	0.5194	0.4556	0.3996	0.3506	0.3075	0.2697
15%	1	0.8696	0.7561	0.6575	0.5718	0.4972	0.4323	0.3759	0.3269	0.2843	0.2472
16%	1	0.8621	0.7432	0.6407	0.5523	0.4761	0.4104	0.3538	0.3050	0.2630	0.2267
17%	1	0.8547	0.7305	0.6244	0.5337	0.4561	0.3898	0.3332	0.2848	0.2434	0.2080
18%	1	0.8475	0.7182	0.6086	0.5158	0.4371	0.3704	0.3139	0.2660	0.2255	0.1911
19%	1	0.8403	0.7062	0.5934	0.4987	0.4190	0.3521	0.2959	0.2487	0.2090	0.1756
20%	1	0.8333	0.6944	0.5787	0.4823	0.4019	0.3349	0.2791	0.2326	0.1938	0.1615

INTERNAL RATE OF RETURN (IRR)

Internal Rate of Return is a very similar method to NPV. It is based on the same concept, but it is a percentage return measure.

With NPV we took the forecasted cash flows for a project and applied a discount factor to calculate an NPV for the project. What if we didn't know the discount factor to use? We could pick a discount factor that would force the NPV to zero. If you like, it's the break-even cost of capital. If interest rates rise and rise, how far do they have to go before the project's NPV = 0 (i.e. the project neither makes nor loses money)?

In order to estimate this value, we can calculate the NPV at a discount factor of 10% as before, then (as both projects were positive at 10%) we could increase the discount factor by a large amount to see if we can force it to a negative NPV. Let's try 30%:

Time	Discount Factor (@ 10%)	Discount Factor (@30%)	Project A				Project B		
			Cash Flow	Discounted Cash Flow (@ 10%)	Discounted Cash Flow (@30%)	Cash Flow	Discounted Cash Flow (@10%)	Discounted Cash Flow (@30%)	
0	1	1	–50,000	–50,000	–50,000	–50,000	–50,000	–50,000	
1	.909	.769	35,000	31,815	26,915	20,000	18,180	15,380	
2	.826	.592	35,000	28,910	20,720	20,000	16,520	11,840	
3	.751	.455				20,000	15,020	9,100	
4	.683	.350				30,000	20,490	10,500	
5	.621	.269				40,000	24,840	10,760	
NPV				10,725	–2,365		45,050	7,580	

The final step is to estimate, using the two values calculated, the point at which the NPV is zero. For Project A, plot the NPV at 10% (i.e. 10,725) and the NPV at 30% (i.e. -2,365) and draw a line between the two. The NPV is zero where the line crosses the x axis at the discount factor of 26%. In other words, at a discount factor of 26%, the NPV is zero and the internal rate of return is 26%.

Do the same for Project B and we see that at both discount factors, the NPVs are positive. Simply plot both values, then extrapolate the line until it crosses the x axis. In this case, this is at 36%; therefore, the IRR of project B is 36%. The cost of capital would have to rise to 36% before the project becomes unviable. This is the better project, as it has the higher IRR. As the IRR is so high, at 36%, we can judge that the project will still be viable if risks occur, so it is a very robust project.

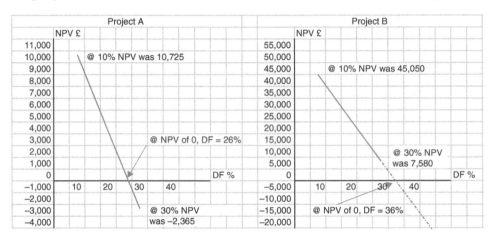

You can download a template from www.TYCoachbooks.com/Finance that will calculate all these values for you.

Benefits

This method is still very reliable as it is based on the same concept as NPV.

Some companies and investors prefer this method as they prefer to see a percentage return.

Drawbacks

There is a flaw in IRR in that it can only calculate an IRR for a single change in direction of cash flow. We need to calculate a separate IRR for every change in direction of cash flow. (The IRR line, unlike the figure above, is actually a curve crossing the DF axis. Each time the direction of cash flows changes, the curve crosses the line again.) So looking at the project below where, for example, a house is bought, then rented out, then requires refurbishment, then returns to positive cash flows, we cannot calculate an IRR for the whole project, because there is technically an IRR for each change in direction of cash flow:

Time	Cash flows
0	−100k
1	25k
2	25k
3	25k
4	−50k
5	25k
6	25k
7	25k
8	25k
9	25k
10	25k

In this case, it is better to rely on the NPV and ignore the IRR.

Why would you use this method?

Many investors like to see a percentage return and therefore prefer an IRR. If you calculate all the measures we've looked at in this section, then your investors or senior managers can make a balanced decision from all the tools available.

COACHING SESSION 20

Review your project investment idea here:

Time	Discount Factor @ ___%	Your Project Cash Flows	Discounted Cash Flow
0	1		
1			
2			
3			
4			
5			
NPV			

ONLINE RESOURCE

A downloadable project evaluation spreadsheet is available at:

www.TYCoachbooks.com/Finance

NEXT STEPS

In this section you have:

* reviewed some example projects using a range of evaluation tools (payback period, Benefit:Cost ratios, return on investment / accounting rate of return, net present value and internal rate of return)

In the next section we will review some specific tools for functional managers.

TAKEAWAYS

This is your opportunity to take stock of what you've learned from this chapter. You might now want to choose other chapters and exercises to focus on, or you can continue to work through the whole book if this better fits your needs.

1. What types of project would you be involved in?

_____

_____

_____

_____

_____

_____

_____

_____

2. Which of the evaluation tools are used in your business? And what are the target rates?

_____

_____

_____

_____

_____

_____

_____

_____

_____

_____

3. Who's support would you need in evaluating your projects and who would need to be involved in the approval process?

_____

_____

_____

_____

_____

_____

_____

_____

_____

_____

4. What have you learned for your next project?

_____

_____

_____

_____

_____

_____

_____

_____

_____

_____

_____

_____

PART 3
FUNCTIONAL SPECIFICS

WHAT SPECIFIC FINANCIAL INFORMATION IS IMPORTANT TO SALES EXECUTIVES?

 OUTCOMES FROM THIS CHAPTER

■ If you're in sales, there are some specific models reviewed in this section just for you.

You may find that sometimes you're not just selling to a direct contact interested in the features and benefits of your product. You may be required to sell a solution to the board who will be more interested in the overall financial impacts of using your solution. Or you may have to work through a procurement professional with some key targets to achieve; they may focus on price reduction unless you can find some other financial benefits to your solution.

If we consider a typical sales process, we can identify where finance has an impact at each stage:

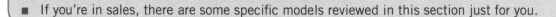

	Sales process steps	Finance impacts
1	Prospecting / initiating contact	Establish company is viable and can pay its bills.
2	Planning the sale	Understand the customer's business model – what financial targets they may have, how will your products or services help them financially?
3	Identifying needs and questioning	Ask customer open questions about needs and financial targets to establish the benefits of your solution.
4	Needs assessment	Establish likely value to the customer of each of your features.
5	Presenting the solution	'You said...' link each need to your service.
6	Negotiation and closing the sale	Negotiating high value / low cost variables.
7	Follow up	Monitor the customer and keep credit control informed.

Let's look at each stage in more detail:

PROSPECTING / INITIAL CONTACT

When first identifying potential customers, it is a good idea to establish their viability before spending a great deal of time establishing a relationship. Your finance business partner can help with this: they can evaluate the company accounts using ratios or buy a report from a credit reference agency to do this for them. If you'd like to know more about how to evaluate potential customers, then chapters 2, 3 and 4 will give you a good overview.

Key figures you'll be interested in are:

- Net profit margin and Return on Capital Employed (ROCE), which will tell you how profitable the potential customer is.

- Debtor days, creditor days, stock days and liquidity ratios will tell you how well your potential customer manages their cash and will tell you about their ability to pay you.

- The gearing ratio will tell you how risky the company is, are they viable in the longer term?

It's important at this stage to work with your credit control department. They will have specific guidelines about payment terms and credit limits depending on the financial status of customers. Find out up front what their criteria are, then provide relevant information to be able to negotiate with them for improved terms for your customer, allowing you more flexibility to trade terms against price to avoid discounting.

For example, if credit control are nervous about a newly formed business unit, you might be able to get a parent company guarantee to give credit control more comfort, allowing them to give a greater credit limit.

Or (for example, with a newly formed company) again credit control may be uncomfortable giving any credit terms; you could negotiate a deposit and payment plan over the following two months as a compromise.

Giving credit controllers information about your customer's targets and growth or new contracts won, for example, may give them more confidence to allow longer payment terms. Remember all this impacts on your company's cash flow, so ensure you trade terms only to maintain price or charge more for your services.

PLANNING THE SALE

Let's understand the potential customer's business model.

- If your customer has a high level of cost of sales / a low gross margin (see chapters 3 and 4), then they will be very price sensitive to any raw materials' purchases.

- If your product has lower wastage / defects, this may be of interest.
- If your product will make their processes more efficient and save them production costs or increase their production throughput, this may be of interest.

- If your customer has a high level of overheads / a low operating margin (see chapters 3 and 4), then they will be price sensitive to any additional overheads.

  - If your product will save overhead costs or make management of their processes easier, this may be of interest.

A key measure for most businesses will be Return on Capital Employed (ROCE) (see chapter 4) which is:

$$\frac{\text{Operating Profit}}{\text{Capital Employed}} \times 100$$

But which can be broken down further:

$$\frac{((\text{Price} - \text{Cost of Sales}) \times \text{Volume} - \text{Fixed Costs})}{(\text{Fixed Assets} + \text{Working Capital})} \times 100$$

To improve their ROCE, your customer could:

- Increase their prices
- Reduce the cost to make their products
- Reduce their overheads
- Reduce the amount of fixed assets they have to use
- Reduce their stockholding
- Reduce their debtor days
- Increase their creditor days

Think about your product or service; what can it do to improve each of these elements for your customer?

Element	Question	Example
Price	Can your product or service help your customer to improve their price?	Can your product bring a higher level of quality to their product? When refitting bathrooms, a hotel may be able to pay more for Jacuzzi baths if this extra facility enables them to improve their 'star rating' and increase their room prices.

Cost of sales	Can your product reduce your customer's cost of sales?	Is your product higher quality with fewer defects or fewer breakdowns / maintenance / refurbishments? If you're selling a car component that needs no replacement during the warranty period, this may reduce ongoing costs.
Volume	Can your product or company help your customer increase volume?	If you're selling machinery that is more efficient than the customer currently uses, you could help them produce more. If you're currently advertising and marketing to a similar customer base, could you do joint marketing activities to help them increase their volume? For example, supermarkets and product brands advertise together and share costs, or brands contribute to a supermarket's advertising where the brand is shown.
Fixed costs (overheads)	Can your product reduce your customer's overhead costs?	If you can sell an automated production management system that monitors and self-corrects, your customer may be able to reduce shift management or supervisory costs.
Fixed assets	Can your product reduce your customer's fixed assets?	Imagine you have a new, more efficient machine that will replace three old-style machines. Despite any higher price, replacing three other machines may be more cost effective. (In addition will there be savings on running costs – *fixed costs?*)
Stock days	Can your lead times reduce the stock your customer needs to hold?	If you are able to deliver reliably and swiftly, or you can sell a year's products up front but have the customer call them off as needed, this will reduce their stockholding.
Debtor days	Can your product reduce debtor days?	If you are able to provide your customer with an automated purchase ordering system for their customers, with credit card or direct debit payment, this may reduce their debtor days (and also reduce their credit control process costs – *fixed costs*).
Creditor days	Can you increase your customer's creditor days?	The obvious solution here is to provide long payment terms to your customer; however, this has a cash impact on your business. Alternative options are: ■ Take credit card payments (which gives you good cash flow but gives the customer extra time to pay their credit card bill). ■ Allow the customer to pay monthly or provide other types of payment plan (at a small cost) to spread their cash flows.

COACHING SESSION 21

Think creatively, what could your product, service or your company do to help your customers to improve their ROCE?

Element	Question	Your solution
Price	Can your product or service help to improve their price?	
Cost of sales	Can your product reduce your customer's cost of sales?	
Fixed costs (overheads)	Can your product reduce your customer's overhead costs?	
Fixed assets	Can your product reduce your customer's fixed assets?	
Stock days	Can your lead times reduce the stock your customer needs to hold?	
Debtor days	Can your product reduce debtor days?	
Creditor days	Can you increase your customer's creditor days?	

IDENTIFYING NEEDS AND QUESTIONING

Alongside your normal questioning to establish customer needs, why not start with a general conversation about their business? You may discover some information that will help you to sell your product or service financially. Let's assume that you probe against each answer given to establish sufficient detail to diagnose their needs and how you can help them:

Example generic questions	Example answers	For your information
How is business?	■ We can hardly cope with demand ■ Sales are in decline ■ Competitors are beating us on price	■ Can you help with efficiency or productivity? ■ Can you help them to increase their price to offset the fall in demand? ■ Can you help them reduce production costs?
What are your key strategic aims?	■ Growth ■ Profitability ■ Innovation	■ Can you help with capacity? ■ Can you help with ROCE (see previous step)? ■ Are there any joint development projects that would benefit you both?
What are your key targets / metrics?	■ Gross margin ⎫ ■ EBIT ■ ROCE ⎬ ■ Growth ⎭	■ See previous step ■ Could joint marketing projects benefit you both?
Other questions you'd like to add….		

NEEDS ASSESSMENT

Once you've established what the customer's general financial issues are, then you can move onto questioning them specifically about the benefits they might see in your product's Unique Selling Points (USPs). For this it would be useful to list all of your USPs. Be very specific: descriptions like better, faster, etc. do not help us to really sell our USPs to the customer. Asking such questions will allow us to target which USPs are of interest to the customer and allow us to focus on talking only about the USPs that they see a benefit in. Customers will feel listened to and that you are tailoring your approach more to their needs.

Example:

Capabilities – How are they different?	Benefits – Why would this be important to the customer?	Questions for customers	Benefits to your company
We have local distribution hubs (our competitors use single national distribution centres).	We can deliver very quickly and on short lead times.	What lead times do your current suppliers quote? How often would you say you have urgent delivery needs? Would it be of benefit to you to be able to reduce your stock holding?	Charge a small premium for urgent deliveries. Avoid discounting by promising small, regular or urgent delivery quantities.
Our production monitoring equipment is fully automated and makes adjustments to production machinery automatically to optimise efficiency.	Customers can reduce production management effort. Production efficiency is optimised.	How much time is spent on monitoring your machinery and adjusting settings? What is the cost of that? How efficient is your production process currently? What impact on costs would perfect efficiency have?	You can provide customers with an ROI, and maximise solution sales. You could price based on savings if you could monitor it.

Adapted from the DVP from TACK International

PRESENTING THE SOLUTION

Just as you would with any feature or benefit, you can explicitly drive home the financial benefits of your solution with a three step model:

1. You said....

2. Our product does...

3. So the benefit to you is....

For example:

You said working capital management was a key metric in your business.

Our local delivery hubs can deliver in half the time of your current provider.

So you can *cut your stockholding by 50%,* reducing your working capital investment by £x.

Or

You said you can hardly cope with demand and need to increase capacity by 50%.

Our machines are three times faster than your existing model.

So you can replace your two machines with one of ours, reducing your fixed asset investment by £x and *reducing your machine operator costs by 50%*.

NEGOTIATING AND CLOSING THE SALE

If you understand the value to the customer of each of your variables and the cost to you of the same, then you can trade variables profitably.

Simply list each variable and the cost to you vs the value to them. Take a look at this example:

Variable	Cost to you	Value to them
Training their engineers	Low	High
Providing a product manual	High	Low
Units painted in their customers' colours	Low	High
Discounts	High	High

If it is simple for you to provide some training for their engineers, but they would place a high value on being able to maintain their equipment themselves, then you should trade this variable against something that is high cost to you.

For example, if they are likely to request a discount, you might include in the initial proposal a cost for training (even though you would normally give it away) then when they request a discount, you could say you're not able to drop the price, but what you could do is give a 25% discount on the training costs. This saves you from discounting the product (high cost to you) but allows you to reduce your training price (low cost to you).

COACH'S TIP

When trading low cost / high value variables, don't give them away all in one go. Small concessions will reaffirm the value in the customer's mind. If you give it away in one go, the customer will realise it wasn't that valuable!

FOLLOW UP

 COACH'S TIP

As you perform your account management role and keeping up relationships with the customer, make sure you maintain a good relationship with your credit controller with a free flow of information (positive and negative news about your customers) to build trust.

If you let credit control know when customers look to be going through difficult times to enable them to prioritise chasing payments, then they will likely trust you more when you give them positive news about other customers you're currently negotiating terms with and they may allow you more flexibility.

 NEXT STEPS

In this section you have:

• Reviewed the financial impacts at each stage of the sales process

In the next section we will review some specific tools for project managers.

 **TAKEAWAYS**

This is your opportunity to take stock of what you've learned from this chapter. You might now want to choose other chapters and exercises to focus on, or you can continue to work through the whole book if this better fits your needs.

1. How could your product, service or your company help your customer improve their ROCE?

_____

_____

_____

_____

_____

_____

_____

_____

2. What are the USPs for your product or service and how will they impact the customer's financial results?

_____

_____

_____

_____

_____

_____

_____

_____

3. What are the costs to you and value to the customer of your key variables?

_____

_____

_____

_____

_____

_____

_____

_____

_____

_____

4. What have you learned from your last negotiation for next time?

_____

_____

_____

_____

_____

_____

_____

_____

_____

_____

_____

14 WHAT SPECIFIC FINANCIAL INFORMATION IS IMPORTANT TO PROJECT MANAGERS?

 OUTCOMES FROM THIS CHAPTER

■ If you're a project manager, there are some specific models reviewed in this section just for you.

Let's review where finance has an impact in a typical project life cycle:

	Project life cycle gate	Financial impact
1	Initiation	Financially evaluate the project costs and benefits.
2	Planning	Budget for the project.
3	Implementation	Manage risks. Manage changes.
4	Monitor and review	Manage the costs.
5	Close and Evaluate	Financial review.

INITIATION

Some project managers are not involved in the financial evaluation of projects prior to the planning stage, they are simply handed the project to manage after approval. Even if you are not involved in this stage, it is important to understand how the project was justified.

During the implementation of the project, things may change, risks may occur and actions will need to be taken to keep the project on track. Sometimes the obvious project management actions do not lead to the best financial results. A good understanding of how projects are evaluated will help you to understand the key financial drivers within the project, this will help you to manage changes during the project.

First, review chapter 12 to understand financial evaluation of projects.

Now, let's review a project's financials and use this to evaluate the impact of changes on the project's results.

Project: table 1

Example Project

Cost of capital = 10%

Description & values	Time 0	1	2	3	4	5	6	7	overall profit
Bid cost	30,000								
Develop new product variant	150,000								
Production costs		7,000,000	7,000,000	7,000,000					
Gen/admin overhead allocation @ 5% of total	9,000	350,000	350,000	350,000					
Contingencies		350,000	350,000	350,000					
Total cost	**189,000**	**7,700,000**	**7,700,000**	**7,700,000**	–	–			
Income		8,085,000	8,085,000	8,085,000	–				
Net	**–189,000**	**385,000**	**385,000**	**385,000**	–	–	–	–	**966,000**
Discount factor	1	0.909	0.826	0.751	0.683	0.621	0.564	0.513	
Present Value	–189,000	350,000	318,182	289,256	–	–	–	–	
Net Present Value								**768,438**	
Internal Rate of Return								**196%**	
Payback period (cum net cash flow)	**–189,000**	**196,000**	**581,000**	**966,000**	**966,000**	**966,000**	**966,000**	**966,000**	**966,000**
Therefore payback occurs in year		1							

Here's an example client project with a cost to bid for the work: it includes a very small up-front development cost to tailor an existing product for the client's needs and a very small margin (5% mark-up on total costs), but luckily, the client will pay monthly on a pro-forma invoice, which keeps the cash flow good.

The evaluation below shows you the overall profit, payback period, net present value and internal rate of return (see chapter 12 for more help with these terms).

As you can see:

- The overall profit is £966,000.

- The NPV is £768,000.

- The IRR is 196% (it's a very small up-front investment, remember).

- Payback occurs in year one.

Now let's make a number of changes to the project to see what impact this will have on the financial results.

Most changes to a project may have additional impacts, so let's look at the impact of just one change at a time to separate out the financial impact at each step.

First, let's assume that income is delayed by 90 days. You may think this is entirely a credit control issue, however imagine that you are missing your milestones, or the client is unhappy with your work and refuses to sign off each milestone or to pay each bill until the milestones are completed to their satisfaction:

As you can see from *Project: table 2,* the impact of this is:

- No impact on overall profit, as you do receive the money eventually.

- NPV is more than halved to £311,000 because of the delay in payment. With this being such a low margin project, delayed cash flow will have a big impact.

- Payback only occurs in year four.

This change has had a big impact on this project. Each project's financial structure is different, so you can't assume that this will be the case for every project. This sensitivity analysis needs to be done for each of your projects individually.

Project: table 2

Example Project									
Description & values		Cost of capital =		10%					
Time	0	1	2	3	4	5	6	7	overall profit
Bid cost	30,000								
Develop new product variant	150,000								
Production costs		7,000,000	7,000,000	7,000,000					
Gen/admin overhead allocation @ 5% of total	9,000	350,000	350,000	350,000					
Contingencies		350,000	350,000	350,000					
Total cost	**189,000**	**7,700,000**	**7,700,000**	**7,700,000**	–	–			
Income		6,063,750	8,085,000	8,085,000	2,021,250				
Net	**−189,000**	**−1,636,250**	**385,000**	**385,000**	**2,021,250**	–	–	–	**966,000**
Discount factor	1	0.909	0.826	0.751	0.683	0.621	0.564	0.513	
Present Value	−189,000	−1,487,500	318,182	289,256	1,380,541	–	–	–	
Net Present Value								**311,479**	
Internal Rate of Return								17%	
Payback period (cum net cash flow)	−189,000	−1,825,250	−1,440,250	−1,055,250	966,000	966,000	966,000	966,000	
Therefore payback occurs in year					4				

Now let's try a different change:

This time, the project is going to run late. Our normal response to this may be to allocate more resources to get the project back on time. In this example, we'll let it run late to see what happens. (See *Project: table 3* for information.)

In this case:

- There is no impact on profit, as we've not allocated extra resources to get the project back on time.

- The NPV is only slightly reduced to £723,000.

- The IRR is still high at 136%.

- The payback has been delayed to slightly later in year one.

All in all, this change has had a much lower impact on the project

The next change we'll try is to have a 5% cost overspend with a fixed income from the client. (Please see *Project: table 4* for this information.)

As you can see, this has had a massive impact:

- The project now makes a loss of £189,000.

- The NPV is now also (£189k) negative (because the whole 5% mark-up is wiped out by the 5% cost overspend).

- The IRR is impossible to calculate.

- The project never pays back.

In this example, because the margin was so low, adding any more cost to the project would be disastrous.

You can see that if the project was over-running and in reaction we added extra resources to get it back on track, this would have been the worst possible decision.

Finally, let's allow the product development phase to over-run and cost double. (Please see *Project: table 5* for this information.)

In this example the impact is not as worrying:

- The overall profit falls a little to £806,000.

- The NPV falls to £538,000.

- The IRR falls to 64%.

- The project pays back in year two.

The impact is low in this example because the development phase of the project is relatively small in cost. In a project with higher development costs, this would be a devastating change.

Project: table 3

Example Project										
	Cost of capital =		10%							
Description & values	**Time**									
	0	1	2	3	4	5	6	7	overall profit	
Bid cost	30,000									
Develop new product variant	150,000									
Production costs		4,000,000	5,000,000	7,000,000	4,000,000					
Gen/admin overhead allocation @ 5% of total	9,000	200,000	300,000	350,000	200,000					
Contingencies		200,000	300,000	350,000	200,000					
Total cost	**189,000**	**4,400,000**	**6,600,000**	**7,700,000**	**4,400,000**	–				
Income		4,620,000	6,930,000	8,085,000	4,620,000					
Net	**–189,000**	**220,000**	**330,000**	**385,000**	**220,000**	–	–	–	**966,000**	
Discount factor	1	0.909	0.826	0.751	0.683	0.621	0.564	0.513		
Present Value	–189,000	200,000	272,727	289,256	150,263	–	–	–		
Net Present Value								723,246		
Internal Rate of Return								136%		
Payback period (cum net cash flow)	–189,000	31,000	361,000	746,000	966,000	966,000	966,000	966,000		
Therefore payback occurs in year	1									

Project: table 4

Example Project	Time								overall profit
	Cost of capital =			10%					
Description & values	0	1	2	3	4	5	6	7	
Bid cost	30,000								
Develop new product variant	150,000								
Production costs		7,350,000	7,350,000	7,350,000					
Gen/admin overhead allocation @ 5% of total	9,000	367,500	367,500	367,500					
Contingencies		367,500	367,500	367,500					
Total cost	**189,000**	**8,085,000**	**8,085,000**	**8,085,000**					
Income		8,085,000	8,085,000	8,085,000					
Net	**–189,000**	–	–	–	–	–	–	–189,000	–189,000
Discount factor	1	0.909	0.826	0.751	0.683	0.621	0.564	0.513	
Present Value	–189,000	–	–	–	–	–	–	–	
Net Present Value								–189,000	
Internal Rate of Return								#NUM!	
Payback period (cum net cash flow)	–189,000	–189,000	–189,000	–189,000	–189,000	–189,000	–189,000	–189,000	
Therefore payback occurs in year					never				

Project: table 5

Example Project	Cost of capital =	10%							
Description & values	**Time**								
	0	**1**	**2**	**3**	**4**	**5**	**6**	**7**	**overall profit**
Bid cost	30,000								
Develop new product variant	150,000	150,000							
Production costs			7,000,000	7,000,000	7,000,000				
Gen/admin overhead allocation @ 5% of total	9,000		350,000	350,000	250,000				
Contingencies			350,000	350,000	250,000				
Total cost	**189,000**	**150,000**	**7,700,000**	**7,700,000**	**7,500,000**	–	–		
Income			8,085,000	8,085,000	7,875,000				
Net	**–189,000**	**–150,000**	**385,000**	**385,000**	**375,000**	–	–	–	**806,000**
Discount factor	1	0.909	0.826	0.751	0.683	0.621	0.564	0.513	
Present Value	–189,000	–136,364	318,182	289,256	256,130	–	–	–	
Net Present Value								**538,204**	
Internal Rate of Return								**64%**	
Payback period (cum net cash flow)	–189,000	–339,000	46,000	431,000	806,000	806,000	806,000	806,000	
Therefore payback occurs in year			2						

COACH'S TIP

Always ask your finance business partner to run through the financial impacts of some typical changes or some of the most likely risks you identified in your risk register to establish what would be appropriate management actions to take in each case. This will help you to establish which of the key financial drivers (ongoing costs, cash, development costs, payment terms, etc.) have the biggest impacts and to make decisions quickly no matter what the situation.

PLANNING

Firstly, take a quick look through chapter 9's departmental budgeting process. Now, let's review the seven step process but in project management terms:

COACHING SESSION 22

Complete the following template with your notes for your project budget:

Step		Notes	Your notes
1	Scope	Determine the scope of the project: ■ What is required? ■ What is outside the scope?	
2	Critical path	Step two is to identify the critical path. Once you've determined the sequence of work plans and what actions are dependent on the completion of other actions, the longest route of dependent actions is the critical path. It must not be delayed without delaying the entire project.	
3	Critical path budget	Budget the resources and costs for the critical path. Defend this part of the budget robustly.	

4	The rest of your budget	Once the critical path is budgeted for, budget for the non-critical path activities and find the most efficient use of resources and timings.	
5	Present and negotiate your budget	In presenting your budget, use the same process: ■ Slide one reminds them of the project scope. ■ Slide two shows the plan, highlighting the critical path. ■ Slide three shows your detailed work plans. ■ Only then should you present the detail of the budget numbers.	
6	Agree the budget	Finalise your agreed budget.	
7	Monitor and review*	Each month, check progress on your operational plans – are you achieving against your time lines, and review your budget – are you on track? If not, what can you do to get back to budget?	

* There are more tools to help with this step in the upcoming section of the project life cycle process step four – monitor and review (manage the costs).

BUDGETING FOR RISKS

QQ COACHING SESSION 23

What risks can you think of that may occur?

How would you normally include a cost for these risks in your budget?

Often people will include a 'guesstimated' contingency figure to cover all the risks, say 10%. This will be difficult to justify and could end up being cut. Instead, try the following process:

1. Gather a team of everyone affected by the budget and brainstorm all the things that could go wrong.

2. Agree the likely cost of each of the risks you've identified. Some risks may have a specific cost, but for others it may be much more difficult to specify a cost. For any risk, use the experience of the whole team:

- Who's encountered a similar risk in the past?

- What were the circumstances?

- What was the cost?

If you can agree a probable cost between the whole team, it is likely to be more accurate than one you have had to estimate on your own.

3. Agree the probability of each risk occurring. You may use a probability percentage or just high / medium / low if you prefer. Again, it is the experience of the team that will make this process more accurate.

Take a look at the example below:

Risk	Cost	Probability	Expected Value
Product development is delayed, 5% extra time is spent	£100,000	25%	£25,000
Product prototype fails, 20% of product requires redesign	£400,000	10%	£40,000
Initial manufacturing wastage and rework higher than anticipated. (1% budgeted, 2% actual costs?)	£50,000	50%	£25,000
Etc....			
Contingency included in budget			£90,000

4. The final step is to multiply the cost by the probability to get an expected value. This is not a TRUE expected value. For example, if the material defects are 2%, then the cost will be £50,000, or £0 if there are no extra defects. However, the idea of the expected value is that over a large number of risks, some will occur, some will not. The overall value of the contingency to be included in the budget is hopefully enough to cover the realised risks as they occur. The important thing is that you've actually thought about the realistic risks and attempted to quantify them, which is better than including a random 10% and more likely to be accepted by senior management and the finance department.

COACH'S TIP

If any of the risks have a probability of 75–80% or above perhaps you should consider taking them out of the risk register and including them directly in the budget. These risks are highly likely to occur. Work package managers who perceive these risks will consider the budget unachievable if they have no contingency budget to cover them. The danger here is that people with perceived unachievable budgets will not even try, and as a consequence perform even worse than if they had no budget at all.

This is a fine balancing act. However, if you put all the contingencies into the main budget, the budget will be perceived as so soft that work package managers may overspend, taking up all the contingency, before any of the risks actually occur.

COACHING SESSION 24

Consider the risks to your budget here:

Risk	Cost	Probability	Expected Value

IMPLEMENTATION

Managing risks

From a financial point of view, managing your risks is mainly concerned with when to release the contingencies from the budget. You'll see from our earlier example that each of the risks was listed in the order in time that they might occur:

Risk	Cost	Probability	Expected Value
Product development is delayed, 5% extra time is spent	£100,000	25%	£25,000
Product prototype fails, 20% of product requires redesign	£400,000	10%	£40,000
Initial manufacturing wastage and rework higher than anticipated. (1% budgeted, 2% actual costs?)	£50,000	50%	£25,000
Etc...			
Contingency included in budget			£90,000

As you work through your project, as each risk is passed without occurring, the temptation for senior management may be to release each contingency figure as this will add directly to the profits shown for the project.

You must however resist attempts to release contingencies too early. Remember, the expected value included in the contingency for each risk is not sufficient to cover that specific risk. If you release each contingency as each risk is passed, when a risk actually occurs you may not have enough contingency in the budget to cover it. Instead, have a discussion at each stage of the project and only release the early contingencies as you reach a point where the remaining risks can be covered by the unreleased contingency.

Managing changes

Your project management processes should include a change management process, including a change request form and a change control log. This chapter is not intended as a project management guide; here we are merely looking at the financial aspects of project management. The key financial point about change management is that any changes, whether requested by the client or required by the project team, may affect the financial results of the project. Ensure that no-one on the project team is authorised to accept and approve change requests without a review of the financial impacts of that change. In step one of this process we saw some 'what if' sensitivity tools to review the impact of changes. You can re-use these spreadsheets to assess the financial impact of changes requested. This way you may be able to renegotiate prices with the client before changes are approved.

MONITOR AND REVIEW

Manage the costs

The key issue in managing costs that makes a project different from any other budget, is the effect of the timing of activities. In a normal departmental budget, we can simply compare budget vs actual costs (see chapter 10 for more information). However, there is another aspect affecting projects; it's not just about 'did we spend more or less than budgeted?' We also have to consider are we ahead of the plan or behind the plan in time? To understand the cost position and the schedule position, we can use the concept of earned value.

Let's review this with a graph:

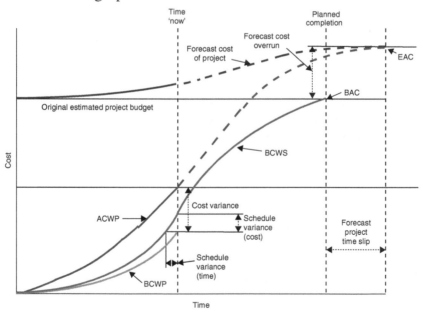

KEY

EAC	Estimate at Completion
BAC	Budget at Completion (current)
BCWS	Budgeted Cost of Work Scheduled (current)
BCWP	Budgeted Cost of Work Performed (earned value)
ACWP	Actual Cost of Work Performed

Source: Hemsley Fraser; Finance for Project Managers

Here you can see we are plotting costs as they are incurred over time.

First look at the line marked BAC, *budgeted cost of work scheduled*. This is your full project budget. The line looks like a flattened S. Most projects will start with lots of planning and little expenditure, then during the main part of the project most of the costs will be incurred, then in the final stages expenditure slows down again as the project is completed.

The line marked BCWP (bottom line) shows us *budgeted cost of work performed*. This is the actual work performed, but not at the actual costs; instead it's at the budgeted cost. The horizontal difference between this line and the BCWS line shows us the amount of time we are behind on this project. The vertical difference between BCWP and BCWS shows us the cost of that schedule variance; how much must we spend (at budgeted rates) to get to where we should be in this project at this time.

The line marked ACWP is the *actual cost of work performed*. The difference vertically between this line and the BCWS is the cost variance, how much have we overspent on our budget so far. If we were looking at a more traditional set of management accounts (see chapter 10) this would be all the variance we would see.

The true full cost variance is the difference vertically between BCWS and ACWP.

The ACWP actual line can be forecast forward including all our latest information to show our latest estimate of the full cost at completion, showing the schedule variance and cost variance expected by the end of the project.

The top (EAC) line is quite simply month on month our latest estimate of the full cost of the project at completion, as we learn more during the project.

CLOSE AND EVALUATE

At the end of most projects, the project team will gather the lessons learned in order to continually improve their project management in future projects. Something that is less commonly done, is to re-calculate the net present value (NPV – see chapter 12 for more information) with the new, known results. This would be a useful exercise to see the full impact of each of the lessons learned, and to improve the financial evaluation exercise at the beginning of the next project.

NEXT STEPS

In this section you have:

- Reviewed the financial impacts at each stage of the project management process

In the next section we will review some specific tools for HR and L&D managers.

TAKEAWAYS

This is your opportunity to take stock of what you've learned from this chapter. You might now want to choose other chapters and exercises to focus on, or you can continue to work through the whole book if this better fits your needs.

1. What have you learned from reviewing the original financial evaluation of your project?

_____

_____

_____

_____

_____

_____

_____

_____

_____

_____

2. What are the key financial drivers for your project?

_____

_____

_____

_____

_____

_____

_____

_____

_____

_____

_____

_____

3. What does this mean for managing your project?

_____

_____

_____

_____

_____

_____

_____

_____

_____

4. What have you learned from presenting your risk register to get your contingency budget approved?

_____

_____

_____

_____

_____

_____

_____

_____

_____

_____

_____

WHAT SPECIFIC FINANCIAL INFORMATION IS IMPORTANT TO HUMAN RESOURCES OR LEARNING AND DEVELOPMENT MANAGERS?

 OUTCOMES FROM THIS CHAPTER

- If you're in HR, there are some specific models reviewed in this section just for you.

Often, human resources (HR) people struggle to gain approval for HR or learning and development (L&D) initiatives, as the benefits are often seen as quite 'soft' and unquantifiable.

Let's review a seven step process that you can use to aid your management team with agreeing their needs, their optimum solutions and establishing the true value of the benefits they seek:

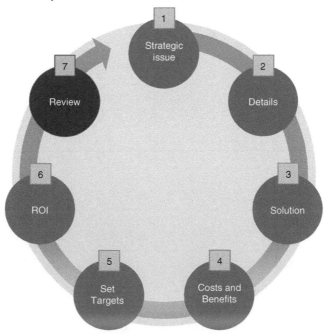

© JSB Group Limited 2014

Step	Details	Example
1. Strategic Issue	The starting point for any discussion about a need for any HR or L&D initiative needs to be either: ■ What is the strategic aim and what is the gap in skills or resources to achieve this aim? or ■ What is the business issue facing us that needs to be resolved?	A technical facilities management company (building maintenance) was struggling to achieve competitive advantage, because in the customers' eyes there was little difference in the technical service provided by any supplier. The chosen route was to focus on exemplary customer service; for contract managers to truly understand their customers' industries and business issues, to provide business advice to get the most out of their assets rather than focusing purely on repairs and planned maintenance, and to build better relationships with the customer to facilitate much more focused bids at contract re-tender highlighting added value services that no other outside competitor could understand.
2. Details	What is the evidence of the need and of the gap? Sometimes data may need to be gathered, at other times anecdotal evidence from the management team will suffice.	Contract managers typically are promoted from an engineering background and need help understanding different industries and business models and help with communication skills to improve customer relationships. Every level of management working at a level below that which they should: contract managers need to act more as account managers, operations managers need to work at a more strategic level, etc. All levels of management need to delegate more responsibility to their direct reports.

| 3. Solution | The solution should be agreed between the whole management team to ensure support.

It is unlikely to be just a training course; it may require a change in objectives, processes, communications, equipment, etc. to ensure the solution works fully.

A good tip is to make sure you do more than you expect you need to to ensure the results are achieved. Belt and braces! | A modular training programme for contract managers covering:

■ communication skills
■ leadership skills
■ business and finance

Supported by more specific e-learning on related topics where required by the contract manager.

Peer-coached specific action planning to use the tools in each module.

Coaching from line managers pre- and post-each module to establish objectives, actions and to follow up on actions taken and support required.

Post-module assignments to discover more about their customers' businesses, map stakeholders, plan communications, present business cases, delegate responsibility, develop their team members, etc.

A change in contract managers' responsibilities to include financial management of contracts and working capital.

A modular leadership programme for operations managers including developmental projects, one of which was to introduce a new personal development review (PDR) process, to improve objective setting, development and delegation across the whole business. |

4. Costs and Benefits	Gather all the costs of the solution plus all the benefits of the solution whether they appear easily quantifiable or are less tangible. If the business need was described in enough detail in step one, this should be easier.	Costs of the training plus coaching time plus the changes in processes and time spent on projects was estimated. The cost of bidding for new business vs the cost of retaining at re-tender time was estimated. An estimate of the average value of new projects sold to existing customers was made. An estimate of the value of delegating 10% of tasks at all levels of management was made.
5. Set Targets	Agree challenging but readily achievable targets with the management team.	Targets were set for: ■ improved contract renewal rates ■ new project sales as a result of the finance and contracts module assignment ■ setting new objectives for staff and delegating 10% of management workloads at each level (allowing growth at zero staffing cost increase).
6. ROI	Use the appropriate measure to suit the project. If there are unquantifiable softer benefits, include them in the presentation as bullet points.	*Review chapter 12 for example project appraisals.*
7. Review	Many organisations fail to review actual project results compared to the original evaluation. If you can gather the data simply and cheaply, it will provide a background of success against which to present future proposals.	Additional business was won from the business case assignments and actual values were tracked. Contract renewal rates are still being tracked (a three year cycle). Anecdotally, greater delegation is occurring but until the implementation of the new PDR process, this is currently not tracked accurately.

Often you might find that the solution is arrived at before the strategic point is explicitly defined. In this case, you can use the same model but work backwards from the solution, asking why, why, why, until you achieve the same results.

Example:

Step 3 (because the solution was already defined, start at step 3, then ask 'why?' to establish steps 1–2). The HR department of a private hospital wanted to put all their 'zero hours contract' non-clinical staff onto permanent contracts at considerable cost.

When asked 'why?', the answer was:

- To improve non-clinical feedback scores from patients.

On further probing it was established that:

- Non-clinical staff are difficult to performance manage as they simply point to permanent staff and ask; 'why should we do more? We don't get the same benefits?'
- Patients receiving food or drinks late or cold are more likely to be critical of clinical staff too.
- Nurses fill the gap and bring food and drinks when they should be focused on nursing.
- Dissatisfied patients don't return, causing a loss in potential revenue.
- Dissatisfied patients cause the best consultants to use different hospitals with better reviews, resulting in a loss in potential revenue.

This information supplies us with all the data we need for *step 1* and the basis to ask questions of the management team for *step 2*:

- Anecdotally, how much time do you believe nursing staff spend on non-clinical duties?
- What are the satisfaction scores for clinical and non-clinical staff?
- Anecdotally, how many consultants do you remember leaving and telling you the reason was the hospital reputation / patient feedback?
- How many non-clinical staff are on zero hours contracts and for how long? And what liabilities might we face as a result?

It is still important to visit *step 3* as simply making non-clinical staff permanent will probably not fix the problem. Changing contracts will not make staff behave differently without having new objectives set, tracked and reviewed. Line managers may need some management training to tackle long term behaviours, etc.

Step 4 involved costing:

- Additional costs of the new permanent contracts.
- Performance management training.
- Management time to implement objectives.

vs

- The benefits of not losing consultants (look at 2–3 consultants lost recently and their revenue in the previous twelve months to estimate an average consultant revenue per year figure).

- Carry out some simple benchmarking of a non-competing private hospital's (from a different region?) satisfaction scores and returning patients.

Step 5 targets:

- A reasonable reduction in consultant losses per year (as agreed by hospital management).

- An achievable satisfaction improvement score and repeat patient visit rate.

- Zero industrial tribunals for long term zero hours employment issues, including unfair dismissal, etc.

COACHING SESSION 25

Have a practise now, before you meet the managers, to give you some ideas to 'get the ball rolling' if needed:

Step	Details	Your ideas:
1. Strategic Issue	■ What is the strategic aim and what is the gap in skills or resources to achieve this aim? or ■ What is the business issue facing us that needs to be resolved?	
2. Details	What is the evidence of the need and of the gap? Sometimes data may need to be gathered, at other times anecdotal evidence from the management team will suffice.	

3. Solution	The solution should be agreed between the whole management team. It is unlikely to be just a training course; it may require a change in objectives, processes, communications, equipment, etc. to ensure the solution works fully.	
4. Costs and Benefits	Gather all the costs of the solution plus all the benefits of the solution whether they appear easily quantifiable or are less tangible.	
5. Set Targets	Agree challenging but readily achievable targets with the management team.	
6. ROI	Use the appropriate measure to suit the project. If there are unquantifiable softer benefits, include them in the presentation as bullet points.	
7. Review	What data can you gather simply and cheaply? How will you do this?	

→ NEXT STEPS

In this section you have:

- Practised using a process to facilitate managers agreeing HR and L&D needs

- Defined the solution, which may have included an HR initiative, a learning intervention, a change in processes, communications, objectives or tools

- Set challenging but achievable targets for improvements

- Calculated costs and benefits and proven a return on your investment

TAKEAWAYS

This is your opportunity to take stock of what you've learned from this chapter. You might now want to choose other chapters and exercises to focus on, or you can continue to work through the whole book if this better fits your needs.

1. What went well in your facilitation of the management meeting to agree HR initiatives' requirements?

_____

_____

_____

_____

_____

_____

_____

_____

2. What could you have done differently for an even better result?

_____

_____

_____

_____

_____

_____

_____

_____

_____

3. What targets were set, how will you most simply track the results?

_____

_____

_____

_____

_____

_____

_____

_____

_____

_____

_____

4. What have you learned for next time?

_____

_____

_____

_____

_____

_____

_____

_____

_____

_____

GLOSSARY OF TERMS

Terminology	Definition
Absorption Costing	A method of accounting for costs that counts the total cost of a product, for example by including a proportion of overheads allocated to each product.
Accounting Period	The period between the publication of financial statements, usually twelve months.
Accounting Rate of Return (ARR)	Also known as the Return on Investment (ROI), this is a project evaluation technique that expresses average annual profit as a percentage of either initial investment or average investment.
Accounts Payable	Also known as creditors. The value of purchases still owed to suppliers by a company.
Accounts Receivable	Also known as debtors. The value of sales still owed to a company by its customers.
Accrual	An accrual is an estimate of a cost incurred where no invoice has been received. It is included in the costs within the Income Statement.
Acquisition	The purchase of an asset – often purchasing a controlling interest in another company.
Adverse Opinion	An audit opinion where the financial statements contain a significant error, therefore are not true and fair.
Amortisation	Spreading the cost of an *intangible* fixed asset (e.g. software) over its useful life. The calculation is the same as for depreciation. However if there is no reliable estimate of life, under FRS 102 the maximum amortisation life should be five years.
Asset	Something a company owns or has control over.
Associated Companies	A company that a parent owns between 20% and 50% of, and has significant influence over.
Audit Report	A report from an independent auditor providing assurance on compliance with accounting standards, usually including the statement that the accounts represent a true and fair view of the state of the business.
Balance Sheet	Also known as the Statement of Financial Position. This is a snapshot at the end of the period showing what a company owns (or controls) and owes.
Borrowings	The capital sum repayable on loans, included in the Statement of Financial Position.

Bottom Line	There is no commonly agreed definition of 'the bottom line'. Managers targeted with gross profit or operating profit may call either of these the bottom line.
	The true bottom line is net profit. This is the last line on the Income Statement showing profit after all costs (cost of sales, overheads and financing costs) are deducted.
Bottom-Up Budgeting	A method of budgeting where everyone budgets for their own area of control and these budgets are consolidated to a total company budget.
Break-Even Analysis	A method of evaluating new business ideas that plots incomes and costs at different levels of output to establish how many products must be sold to neither make a profit nor a loss.
Budget	A quantitative statement for a defined period of time, which may include planned revenues, assets, liabilities and cash flows.
	Source: CIMA Global
Called-Up Share Capital	The number of shares issued multiplied by the nominal value of the shares (the shares may have been sold for more than the nominal value, so this is not the full receipt for sales of shares).
Capital	The investment made by shareholders in a business.
Capital Expenditure (CapEx)	Expenditure on non-current assets (fixed assets).
Capitalise	To account for the purchase of a fixed asset on the Statement of Financial Position. The item will be depreciated over its useful life through the Income Statement.
Cash and Cash Equivalents	The closing balance of cash and short term accessible investments (e.g. balance in the current account) included in the current assets on the Statement of Financial Position.
Cash Flow Forecast	A plan of cash inflows and outflows for a future period produced for the purposes of cash management and control.
Cash Flow Statement	A financial statement showing a reconciliation from operating profit to net cash flow for a defined period of time (usually twelve months).
Component Accounting	When a complex asset is purchased (e.g. a building), different parts of the building will be depreciated over different lives (for example the windows will not last as long as the main structure – bricks and mortar).
Consolidated Accounts	A group must publish consolidated accounts for all the entities within the group.

Contingent Liability	A contingent liability is an amount a company will possibly owe, if a certain situation occurs. For example the cost of litigation damages is contingent on losing the case. The details relating to a contingent liability are discussed in the notes to the financial statements but not actually recognised as a liability.
Contribution	The surplus of income over purely variable costs. It is an abbreviation of 'contribution towards fixed costs'.
Cost:Benefit Analysis (or Benefit:Cost)	A project evaluation technique that compares total incomes to total costs for any project. Where incomes exceed costs, the project is approved.
Cost of Capital	The true cost of capital employed is the cost of interest and dividends expressed as a percentage of loans and equity. More often companies will estimate a cost of capital greater than this true figure and use it as a target for evaluating investment opportunities. The reason for increasing the figure used from the true cost is to ensure that if interest rates fluctuate a buffer is provided, to cover risk and to ensure investments approved provide a greater profit than just the cost of capital.
Cost of Sales (COS) or Cost of Goods Sold (COGS)	A figure from the Income Statement matching the direct costs of all goods or services sold with the revenue recognised. As a rough guide, anything that touches the product or service is included in Cost of Sales, other costs will be categorised as overheads.
Creditors	Also known as accounts payable. The value of purchases still owed to suppliers by a company.
Current Asset	Something owned or controlled by a company but to be kept/ used for less than one year (for example, inventory, accounts receivable, cash).
Current Liabilities	Something owed by a company and due to be paid in less than one year (for example, creditors, overdraft).
Debt	The sum of all amounts owed to other parties.
Debtors	Also known as accounts receivable. The value of sales still owed to a company by its customers.
Depreciation	Spreading the cost of a tangible fixed asset over its useful life. It is an estimate of the cost incurred in using an asset, spread evenly throughout many Income Statements to match the cost fairly against revenues earned from the asset.
Discount Factor	A percentage cost of capital (or hurdle rate) used to discount future cash flows for a project in the financial evaluation of investments.
Dividend	A discretionary payment to shareholders, sharing the net profit proportionately amongst the shareholders.

Earnings per Share (EPS)	The net profit divided by the number of shares in issue.
EBIT	Also known as operating profit. A profit figure from the Income Statement showing revenues minus all Cost of Sales and overheads, but before financing costs.
EBITDA	Profit before interest, tax, depreciation and amortisation. This figure can be used internally as a target for managers as it shows revenue minus only controllable costs. It can also be used in a valuation for acquiring a business (EBITDA x industry multiple).
Equity	Funds attributable to shareholders: capital invested plus retained earnings.
Expenses	Also known as overheads. Costs not directly attributable to the production of goods or provision of services.
Factoring	Selling your accounts receivable to an outside company to release cash. You will likely be paid less than the face value of the accounts receivable. The purchaser will chase the debts and hope to collect more than they paid you.
Finance Lease	A financial loan to fund the purchase of equipment that is used in the business. At the end of the lease term, the equipment is usually retained by the lessee.
Financial Accounts / Financial Statements	Accounts legally required to be published for a company, where the methods of accounting for income and costs must comply with accounting standards.
Finished Goods	Part of inventory, the value of completed products or finished work not yet delivered or invoiced to the customer.
Fixed Asset	Also known as non-current asset. Something owned or controlled by a company and expected to be kept/used for more than one year (for example; buildings, machinery, vehicles).
Fixed Cost	A cost that does not vary in proportion to output (for example rent, management salaries).
Fraud	A fraud is when the financial statements are deliberately misstated (fraudulent financial reporting), or it can mean theft of company assets, including cash.
FRS 102	An accounting standard published by the UK Financial Reporting Council (FRC) with which most UK businesses (except very small companies and plcs) must comply.

Gearing	The level of long term loans as a percentage of total capital employed. It is a measure of risk: high gearing is risky because a company with a large proportion of loans, if suffering a drop in sales and profits, may struggle to pay the high fixed cost of interest.
Going Concern	A business is a going concern if it will continue in operational existence for the foreseeable future.
Goodwill	The price paid to acquire a business less the value of the net assets of that business. This figure is included in the Statement of Financial Position to reflect the difference between the cash paid out to acquire a business and the net assets bought. It is a balancing figure.
Gross Profit	Sales revenue less costs of goods sold.
Group	A number of companies under the control of a parent or holding company.
Hedging	Reducing risk by taking out a financial contract to offset risks. For example, if selling goods overseas in the future, you could make a separate financial transaction to buy the same value of foreign currency in the same future time at today's values to offset any currency value fluctuations.
Holding Company	The ultimate company owning others in a group. The holding company is not a trading entity (unlike a parent company).
Hurdle Rate	A percentage cost of capital (or discount factor) used to discount future cash flows for a project in the financial evaluation of investments.
IAS	International Accounting Standards – also known as IFRS – see below.
IFRS (International Financial Reporting Standards)	A set of accounting standards published by the International Accounting Standards Board (IASB) with which listed companies in Europe must comply.
Impairment	An amount written off an asset due to a significant fall in value; for example, if a property is physically damaged or an investment loses its value due to a stock market crash.
Income	Also known as revenue, sales or turnover. Income from sales of goods or services.
Income Statement	Also known as the profit and loss account, income and expenditure account (in not-for-profit organisations) or statement of operations (in the US). This is a statement of all income and expenditure for a set period (usually twelve months).
Incremental Budgeting	A method of budgeting where the starting point is either last year's budget or last year's actual income and costs, then changes are made to this base point to reflect any changes in the new year's plan.

Intangible	Something which cannot be touched (e.g. software, goodwill). Intangible non-current assets will be amortised. If there is no reliable estimate of life, under FRS 102 the maximum amortisation life should be five years.
Internal Controls	Activities performed that should ensure that balances and transactions are correctly accounted for.
Inventory	A stock of goods held to be sold. This can be raw materials, work in progress or finished goods.
Investment	Where a company owns less than 20% of the shares of another.
IRR (Internal Rate of Return)	A project evaluation technique that involves discounting future cash flows from a project by a percentage that ensures the net present value is 0. It is the break-even cost of capital of a project. It shows that if interest rates increase, at what cost of capital we would no longer approve the project.
ISA	International Standards on Auditing – the requirements and guidance followed by external auditors
KPI (Key Performance Indicator)	A financial or non-financial measurement used to target teams' or individuals' performance.
Leverage	Also known as gearing. The level of non-current debt as a percentage of total capital employed. It is a measure of risk: high gearing is risky because a company with a large proportion of loans, if suffering a drop in sales and profits, may struggle to pay the high fixed cost of interest.
Liability	A present obligation arising from past events that will result in a cash outflow from the business.
Liquidity	The level of cash available in the business to pay liabilities.
Management Accounts	Internal detailed statements of budgeted vs actual incomes and costs for the purposes of control.
Management Letter	A report provided by the auditor to the company that outlines problems found during the audit and recommends improvements to be made.
Margin	A margin is any profit line as a percentage of sales income. Examples are gross margin, operating margin, net margin, etc.
Marginal Costing	A method of costing used for decision making that only counts the costs incurred as a direct result of a decision (i.e. not including overheads that will be incurred irrespective of the decision).
Margin of Safety	In break-even analysis, the difference between planned sales and the break-even volume of sales. How much can planned sales fall before we no longer make a profit?

Medium Company (or medium group)	To be a medium-sized company (or group), the criteria of a Small Company must not be met and at least two of the following conditions must be met: <ul><li>Annual turnover must be £25.9 million or less</li><li>The Statement of Financial Position total must be £12.9 million or less</li><li>The average number of employees must be 250 or fewer.</li></ul>
Non-Controlling Interest	The portion of a business not held by the controlling parent company.
Negative Goodwill	Where a business is bought for less than its net asset value, this is the difference between the price paid and the net asset value.
Negative Working Capital	When current assets are less than current liabilities. This may indicate a liquidity problem (the company cannot pay its short term liabilities) or it may indicate a business model whereby the company utilises creditors' cash to fund the short term operations of the business.
Net Assets	Total assets less total liabilities.
Net Book Value	The value included in the Statement of Financial Position for each non-current asset, calculated as the original cost of the asset less accumulated depreciation.
Net Profit	Also known as profit after tax. The 'bottom line' profit figure after all costs are deducted from revenue. This profit is attributable to shareholders and may be paid out to shareholders as dividends.
Non-Current Asset	Also known as fixed asset. Something owned or controlled by a company and expected to be kept/used for more than one year (for example, buildings, machinery, vehicles).
Non-Current Liability	Something owed by a company, but due to be paid after more than one year (for example a long term loan).
Non-Recurring Cost (NRC)	A one-off cost, often incurred at the start of a project; for example, research and development.
NPV (Net Present Value)	A project evaluation technique that totals up the up-front investment and future net cash flows arising from a project. All the cash flows are stated in today's money terms by discounting the future cash flows by a discount factor reflecting the cost of capital.
Operating Expenditure (OpEx)	Expenditure on day to day running costs to be included in the overheads section of the Income Statement.
Operating Lease	Rental of equipment, often short term, where the equipment is not owned by you and will be returned to the lessor at the end of the lease term.

Operating Profit	Also known as EBIT (Earnings before Interest and Tax) this is a profit figure from the Income Statement showing revenues minus all cost of sales and overheads, but before financing costs.
Overdraft	A short term agreement with a bank allowing you to spend more money than is currently in your account.
Overheads	Also known as expenses. Costs not directly attributable to the production of goods or provision of services.
Parent Company	The ultimate company owning others in a group. The parent is also a trading entity.
Payback Period	A project evaluation technique that shows in terms of time, how long it takes for a project's net cash inflows to equal the up-front investment. The project's payback period is compared to a company set target, for example three years.
P/E ratio (Price:Earnings ratio)	The share price divided by the earnings per share.
Profit and Loss Account	Also known as the Income Statement, income and expenditure account (in not-for-profit organisations) or statement of operations (in the US). This is a statement of all income and expenditure for a set period (usually twelve months).
Provision	A provision (a recognition of an uncertain liability) must be made in the accounts when: ■ The company has an obligation at the reporting date. ■ It is probable that the company will have to pay. ■ The amount of the obligation can be reliably estimated.
Raw Materials	Part of inventory, the value of unprocessed stock.
Recurring Cost	A cost that will occur continuously over a period of time (for example, rent or raw materials).
Re-Forecasting	A process of re-budgeting at set points throughout the year (half-yearly or quarterly) to make sure targets are still valid and to allow investor relations staff to communicate the latest position to the shareholders.
Reserves	An accumulation of retained profits included in the equity section of the Statement of Financial Position.
Retained Profit	Profits retained in the business, not paid out as dividends to shareholders. This figure is accumulated in the reserves within the Statement of Financial Position.

Revaluation	Assets can be revalued to fair values, but if revalued once they must be revalued regularly to ensure the fair value is kept up-to-date (changes in valuation are reflected in the equity section of the Statement of Financial Position or in the Income Statement depending on the type of asset that is being revalued).
Revenue	Also known as sales, income or turnover. Income from sales of goods or services.
ROCE	Return on Capital Employed. A measure of profitability against investment. There is no agreed calculation, it could be operating profit or net profit as a percentage of total equity plus long term borrowings, or as a percentage of total assets less current liabilities, for example.
ROI (Return on Investment)	More correctly known as the Accounting Rate of Return (ARR), this is a project evaluation technique that expresses average annual profit as a percentage of either initial investment or average investment.
RONA (Return on Net Assets)	A measure of profitability against investment. Either operating profit or net profit as a percentage of total assets less total liabilities.
ROTA (Return on Total Assets)	A measure of profitability against investment. Either operating profit or net profit as a percentage of total assets.
Sales	Also known as revenue, income or turnover. Income from sales of goods or services.
Semi-Fixed Cost (or Semi-Variable Cost)	A cost made which partially varies in proportion to output and is partially fixed (e.g. electricity costs: standing charge plus per Kw/hour costs).
Share Premium	The difference between the price shares are sold for and the nominal value of those shares. (Shares cannot be sold at a discount).
Small Company (or Small Group)	To be a small company (or small group), at least two of the following conditions must be met: ■ Annual turnover must be £6.5 million or less. ■ The Statement of Financial Position total must be £3.26 million or less. ■ The average number of employees must be 50 or fewer. Small companies have exemptions to publishing accounts: they publish abbreviated accounts.

Solvency	The ability of a business to meet its long term liabilities.
Standard Costing	A method of accounting for costs that involves budgeting a standard value for every direct and indirect component of a product and using this value as a 'standard' cost in the actuals included in internal management accounts. At period ends, corrections need to be made for variances to budget (or under-over-absorptions). Standard costing allows managers to control volumes against budget where they have no control over procurement prices.
Statement of Cash Flows	A financial statement showing a reconciliation from operating profit to net cash flow for a defined period of time (usually twelve months).
Statement of Comprehensive Income	A financial statement showing the profits made by the change in values of assets; for example, pension funds, financial assets, revaluation of assets to their fair value, etc.
Statement of Financial Position	Also known as the balance sheet. This is a snapshot at the end of the accounting period showing what a company owns (or controls) and owes.
Stock	An inventory of goods held to be sold. This can be raw materials, work in progress or finished goods.
Subsidiary	A company that a parent company owns 51% or more of and therefore controls.
Substantive Procedure	A type of procedure carried out by the external auditor when conducting their investigation into the financial statements.
Tangible	Anything that can be touched.
Top-Down Budgeting	A method of budgeting where senior people set the budget and allocate income and cost targets to their teams.
Transfer Price	The price at which companies sell products or services to other companies within the same group.
True and Fair	The audit opinion given on a set of financial statements that are free from significant error.
Turnover	Also known as sales, income or revenue. Income from sales of goods or services.
UK GAAP	United Kingdom Generally Accepted Accounting Principles. A main component of UK GAAP is FRS 102 – see above.
US GAAP	United States Generally Accepted Accounting Principles. A set of accounting standards with which US businesses must comply.
Variable Cost	A cost which varies directly in proportion to output (for example, raw materials).
Variance	The difference between budget and actual costs or incomes, shown in internal management accounts.

WACC (Weighted Average Cost of Capital)	The true cost of capital employed is the cost of interest and dividends expressed as a percentage of loans and equity. More often companies will estimate a cost of capital greater than this true figure and use it as a target for evaluating investment opportunities. The reason for increasing the figure used from the true cost is to ensure that if interest rates fluctuate a buffer is provided, to cover risk and to ensure investments approved provide a greater profit than just the cost of capital.
WIP (Work in Progress)	Part of inventory, the partially processed materials or partially complete work.
Working Capital	Current assets less current liabilities. This is the amount of cash required to keep the business operating day to day.
Zero Based Budget (ZBB)	A method of budgeting that takes no account of past performance, instead starting with a blank sheet of paper and determining the objectives, processes, resources, income and costs for a future time period.

BIBLIOGRAPHY

Chapter 1 – What information is available on company performance and where might I find it?

- Other published info: Companies Act 2006.

Chapter 5 – I need to feel confident looking at accounts for businesses in very different industries.

- Extracts from published accounts and notes for:
    - The BBC
    - ITV
    - Sky

Chapter 7 – I have an audit coming up.

- Definition of an audit taken from 'Audit Quality Fundamentals – Audit Purpose' (July 2006, ICAEW Audit and Assurance Faculty, p. 9).

Chapter 13 – What specific information is important to sales executives?

- USP finder; adapted from the 'Differentiated Value Proposition' by TACK International.

Chapter 14 – What specific financial information is important to project managers?

- 'Earned Value Chart', Hemsley Fraser Group Ltd.

Chapter 15 – What specific financial information is important to Human Resources or Learning and Development Managers?

- '7 stages from Business issue to Financial justification', JSB Group Ltd.

Section 4 – Glossary of Terms.

- Budget definition, CIMA Global.

INDEX